"There are a zillion books written by pasto[r]
But I know of no book like the one Erdm[an]
'practical theology'—practical in that it
of the bodily life of the church, theological because here is a pastor
who is theologically informed and who knows how to move from the
tradition to the reality of the church. For those who know that God is
doing 'a new thing,' this is the book, for Erdman shows how we may be
participants in that new thing that God is working among us. The book
is filled with courage and discernment that will be informative. More
than that, readers will find it empowering."

—**Walter Brueggemann,** Columbia Theological Seminary

"This is a practical, vibrant, experience-based book about preaching.
It arises out of critical and reflective practice and is written with com-
pelling honesty. But it would be a mistake to look upon *Countdown to
Sunday* as a 'how-to' book. The author risks violating some of the canons
of homiletics, shakes up cherished assumptions, and ignites hard but
productive thinking about the task and practice of preaching."

—**Darrell L. Guder,** Princeton Theological Seminary

"*Countdown to Sunday* takes us through the weekly practices and rhythms
of a pastor who rejects canned sermon preps and prefabricated mul-
timedia in favor of a high-wire act of living with and leaning against
the Word of God in advance of the Sunday sermon. By turns wry and
unsparing, down-to-earth and profound, this book is a reaffirmation of
the preacher's calling in the best sense. A first-rate book for preachers
and congregations alike."

—**Michael L. Budde,** DePaul University

"Chris Erdman has written a book on preaching that's wise, honest
about the struggle, and immensely inviting. He calls on us preachers
to respect scripture's 'mischief-making' ways among our congregations, and in doing this, he reminds us of our true vocation and the
only thing we're given to perform our prophetic roles. We're given
words. We tell the truth about God. How antiquated! How quaint!
No, how powerful."

—**Sharon Huey,** Grace Fellowship Community Church,
San Francisco

"A key issue for leaders seeking to cultivate missional life is how to
communicate—how to shape and engage people in and with the Word
in ways that invite imagination and transformation. There are no
simple, quick answers. It is a journey and discipline in which we need

wise, experienced guides. I have known Chris for many years. He is a seasoned pastor who has learned the skills of shaping the preaching discipline. I highly recommend this book."

—**Alan Roxburgh,** author of *Crossing the Bridge: Church Leadership in a Time of Change* and *The Sky Is Falling: Leaders Lost in Transition*

"Here's a book born out of the conviction and daily life of one who possesses great skill and a daring heart to train preachers for their task today. I've read many books on preaching, but this one has informed and transformed me like no other. It's a practical and timely manual for pastors, evangelists, students—and those who teach them—who are sent to preach God's Word and bring healing to their communities . . . in America, in Africa, and everywhere else."

—**Bekele Bedada,** Meserete Kristos Church, Addis Ababa, Ethiopia

"Erdman has written a modern classic not only on preaching but on the whole journey of faith in today's world. It resonates both with our vulnerable yet strong humanity and with the God who understands so profoundly the contradictions of the human spirit. Let me put it quite simply: this is a truly great book—one not to read in a hurry. You'll want to keep it beside you over weeks and months, even years."

—**Peter Millar,** theologian, activist, and a former warden of The Iona Community, Scotland

"Chris Erdman invites those who preach to let the truth bleed through their sermons. *Countdown to Sunday* is itself a blood transfusion for preachers running low on energy for the weekly call to speak the Word."

—**Edwin Searcy,** University Hill Congregation, United Church of Canada, Vancouver, BC, Canada

"In an age when many churches seem to want 'personality' in their preachers and pep-talk sermons from their pulpits, *Countdown to Sunday* explores the deeper mysteries, challenges, and joys of the preaching life. Drawing on two decades of pastoral experience—and unafraid to scrutinize his own homiletical failures—Erdman writes wisely of the daily disciplines necessary to sustain the art and practice of sermon writing. More than a book for and about preachers, *Countdown to Sunday* reminds us that preaching is not so much about crafting a clever sermon as it is about the preacher and congregation together shaping a shared witness for the sake of the gospel and the world."

—**Debra Dean Murphy,** author of *Teaching That Transforms: Worship as the Heart of Christian Education*

Countdown
to Sunday

Countdown to Sunday

A Daily Guide
for Those Who Dare to Preach

Chris Erdman

 **Brazos**Press
Grand Rapids, Michigan

© 2007 by Chris Erdman

Published by Brazos Press
a division of Baker Publishing Group
P.O. Box 6287, Grand Rapids, MI 49516-6287
www.brazospress.com

Printed in the United States of America

Library of Congress Cataloging-in-Publication Data
Erdman, Chris William
    Countdown to Sunday : a daily guide for those who dare to preach / Chris Erdman.
        p. cm.
    ISBN 10: 1-58743-203-X (pbk.)
    ISBN 978-1-58743-203-3 (pbk.)
    1. Preaching. I. Title.
BV4221.E73 2007
251—dc22   2007004926

To my father—
who first taught me the power of words

Contents

9

11

Introduction

In differing degrees of intensity, each of us who preach knows at a gut level that the world is becoming an increasingly difficult and even intimidating place for us to preach the gospel. If we're not intimidated by the tricks and technologies of popular, super-success communicators, we're troubled by the apathy and anxiety of dwindling congregations or by the turmoil of this post-9/11 world and the difficulty of trying to find our bearings in the midst of it.

North American preachers haven't always faced what we preachers face today. There was a time when preachers could assume that, while not all North Americans were on the same page, most were at least reading from the same Book. The Bible enjoyed enormous authority, and therefore so did its preachers. In those days, the church lived essentially at the center of North American culture and enjoyed a genuine sense of established power and privilege. But today, the church is increasingly disestablished, decentered, and marginal; even the once-mainline churches are gasping for air, grasping for the privilege they once enjoyed. And in spite of the apparent centeredness of civil religion current in American politics, many thoughtful Christians experience the growing uneasiness that genuine Christian conviction and practice are becoming strange and often unwelcome to those around us.

Now is not an easy time for us to preach the Bible and form congregations responsive to what the Bible calls us to do and be in the world. But when was preaching ever a safe task for the prophets and apostles of the Word? When was the formation of evangelical communities ever met with accolades by a society's powers? Preaching that is safe and easy is quite simply not preaching. Safe and easy preaching is a domestication of the Word of God, a seduction of the preacher's calling by the Sirens of the age, and a subordination of the preacher's daring speech to forms of speech more "relevant" to consumer appetites or more useful to the global interests of the imperialists. There's plenty of foolishness afoot among North American preachers today who are trying to make sense of the dizzying shifts in Western culture and the many temptations that attend them.

In this little book, my aim is to examine the day-to-day life of one who dares to preach in this day and age. *Examine* may not be the right word, for what I'm doing here is larger than that. This isn't a distanced study of the work we preachers do; it's more a testimony from one who's been preaching for most of these last two decades of tumultuous change.

Much of what I've written here was written without a book in mind. These essays or meditations were often written first thing Thursday mornings as I got myself ready to write a sermon each week. I told myself that I was writing them for my preaching students—for I have found that what energizes my students most is when their questions about the daily work of preaching carry me past my teaching notes for the day and into stories and convictions that come from my daily life as a pastor. But even as I wrote these meditations for my students, I found that these words were as much for me as they were for them. During the days and weeks and years since that fateful day of September 11, 2001, these meditations helped me not only keep my bearings in an increasingly tumultuous world, but also to articulate what I really believe about preaching examined through what I do on a daily basis among and for the people I love and serve with the Word of God.

As they stand, these meditations cover everything from exegesis and sermon preparation to how preachers open the Bible in hospitals, from how preachers might preach after a disaster like Hurricane Katrina to what it might mean to host the text as American troops are rolling into Baghdad. They are brief and don't need to be read in any particular order. Some, like my meditations on "Preaching and War" and "Preaching Jesus up against the Jesus of Suburbia," are decidedly provocative. Many chapters explore the soul of the preacher as much as they explore technique. All of them press for an ethic of preaching that cannot be divorced from a working, on-the-ground theology of preaching.

And so, I aim to offer this testimony as a preacher among preachers, and one who hopes my efforts help form a generation of preachers who find in these brief chapters a companion, a dialogue partner, a provocateur with whom they can profitably agree and rigorously disagree, all the while forming their own lives and practices as preachers of the Word of God. I hope that this little book might be, for a season, a daily partner in the life of solitary preachers

15

who know they cannot do this work alone. I also hope it is read and debated in classrooms of students and among groups of pastors who are together finding new courage and joy in their work, increasingly capable of resisting the pressure to lend their voices to the lesser powers that would just as soon claim and use them. "As persons sent from God and standing in his presence" (2 Corinthians 2:17), I pray this little book helps us animate a new and daring trust in the power of the gospel and a fresh urgency to bind every ounce of energy toward the task of tending the Word of God in such a way that the scripture-shaped congregations we serve can embody the kingdom of God and call all the world around them to conversion.

I also offer this book with a deep sense of gratitude toward three key communities who've made this possible. First, for the congregation called University Presbyterian Church; they are home to my wife, Julie, my sons, Josh and Jeremy, and to me. They are the ones who give shape to our lives as much as we give shape to theirs. We're in this preaching business together, and I'm not merely their preacher; because of what we're learning together we are becoming a preaching congregation—a people whose very life together gives evidence to the truthfulness of the gospel. Thanks too for staff colleagues, Ken Johnson and Justin Spurlock, who gave the final manuscript the gift of their good editorial eye and their ability to see when I was being true to the way all this works itself out in our local setting and when I was not. Second, I give thanks for the students and faculty at Mennonite Brethren Biblical Seminary. That a Reformed pastor teaches among Anabaptists is evidence enough of the school's particularly missional vision, so necessary in today's world. They not only put up with my unusual ideas and sometimes strange ways of teaching today's preachers, but actually celebrate them. And third, as yet one more witness to the mischief of God, I give thanks to the community of Roman Catholic sisters and brothers who let me work away for a few hours each week at a table at the Holy Child Monastery Bookstore in Fresno, California. It's there that I spend my Thursday mornings writing my sermons. And it's there that most of this book was written. So, Reformed, Anabaptist, and Roman Catholic forms of Christianity have all, in one way or another, conspired to offer this testimony for the sake of the church's preaching in the challenging years to come and which are already upon us.

Chris Erdman
July 15, 2006
The Feast of St. Bonaventure (1221–1274),
teacher of that little band of daring preachers
known as the Franciscans

1

Why Preaching Requires Blood

There is a Hasidic tale that reveals, with amazing brevity, both the universal tendency to want to be someone else and the ultimate importance of becoming one's self: Rabbi Zusya, when he was an old man, said, "In the coming world, they will not ask me: 'Why were you not Moses?' They will ask me: 'Why were you not Zusya?'"

Parker Palmer
Let Your Life Speak: Listening for the Voice of Vocation

Those of us who preach know how tempted we are to be someone else, wear masks, and live inside our own skin in ways that are not altogether authentic. The demands of pastoral ministry are many and diverse, and while tending the souls of others and the life of a congregation it's not hard to betray our own selves. We stand up on Sunday mornings in a place that can often feel more like a place of danger than a sanctuary. Conflict over a decision of

19

the board, the pain of a family in crisis, the desires of those who hope you'll tilt the church in the direction of their hopes and dreams, your own lingering mistakes and self-doubts and private cravings load the room where you stand to preach; it's little wonder that we wear masks. It's possible to preach in such a way that we keep these masks intact. But I don't think we can keep them intact and preach *Christianly*. Christian preaching is, among other things, an announcement of the new creation, a whole new humanity in Jesus Christ, a liberation from old captivities. When we wear masks, preaching becomes more about technique and the arts of rhetoric and oratory—managing those masks with greater skill—than it is about entering God's new world made real through preaching. And preaching, if it is to be Christian, requires real humanness—God's own in Jesus Christ, and ours as his witnesses, as scandalous as that may be.

Practicing pastors and students alike are often naive about our masks—though we all know the weight of them. We think the way forward is through better technique, greater control, and expertise. We want methods to guide our growth, guarantee our competence, and earn respect. We want to be someone else . . . Moses . . . or, for me, Ed Searcy. We think we can live and preach from inside the half-light of falsehood. But from behind our masks we cannot be as truthful as the gospel invites us to be, as truthful as our congregations need us to be.

What I'm talking about is not mere self-actualization; preaching isn't primarily *about* us. "We do not proclaim ourselves," Paul taught. "We proclaim Jesus Christ as Lord and ourselves as your slaves for Jesus' sake" (2 Corinthians 4:5). Relinquishing our masks isn't about developing a public persona, a radiant personality, even a well-adjusted self. It's not about sharing more stories about ourselves with the congregation. It's about dying to all that makes us false, letting the Sunday text strip us down, carry us under the waters of our baptism, and rising newborn—witnesses of a w/hol(l)y different life. Preaching is about forming congregations who can do the same and who become living witnesses to the newness of God—*preaching* congregations who are themselves open, unmasked, unadorned clay jars through whom the treasure of the gospel shines brightly (2 Corinthians 4). Humanness, finally and scandalously naked and unmasked, is the bearer of the glory of God. And if congregations are ever to drop their own masks and enter the mystery and marvel of this nakedness, then their preachers will have to lead the way.

Dropping our masks is a fearful and often painful journey that runs counter to so much around us. We'd easier speak what we think is expected of us, not what we know and feel in those deep, scripture-soaked places where truth resides. The truth is costly. It is not safe. It runs up against the powers of death that would sooner have us cocooned inside safe, gated communities or behind safe, gated sermons that comfort people and assure them that their desire to live long, wealthy, and healthy lives is just what the gospel wants them to have—all the while living lives locked inside a banal existence, terrified by death, and supporting anything and anyone that will promise to keep them safe. Our preaching wants to run counter to all this, but it won't unless we are willing to speak what we feel deep inside to be true, to bleed for this truth, to put our lives on the line.

If we do, if we take that risk, we will not be alone. The prophets rarely said what the powers wanted them to say; instead they dropped their masks, opened a vein,

21

and bled for God. The apostles, by and large, were not skilled orators; they dropped their masks, opened a vein, and bled for God. Jesus confounded the expectations of the mask-wearers and mask-bearers and spoke with a new authority because he dared to speak the truth regardless of the cost; he opened a vein and bled for God.

Artists and writers know this truth too. Michelangelo, Van Gogh, Picasso, Mozart, Tolstoy, Shakespeare, Twain, Faulkner, Steinbeck, Bob Dylan, Ray Charles, Johnny Cash. They know better than to try to put on what is not theirs. They know that when they try to be someone else, it rings hollow . . . false. It wasn't until they entered fully into the humanness breathed into them by God that these artists found their genius. They stopped trying to be Moses. Picasso, Twain, and Cash entered into the wonder of their own God-breathed originality, and they shook the world. They found the freedom that comes whenever a person is daring enough to speak from the truthfulness of a heart willing to bleed.

Blood heals . . . in more ways than one. We who preach Jesus Christ know this better than anyone else. Preaching—if it is going to heal us from the lies and falsehoods we too easily purchase as truth and from all that wounds us and the world so deeply—preaching, if it is to be Christian, is going to have to cost us.

And the first thing it will cost us is our falsehood, our own masks.

2

"How?" Is Not the Question That Gets Us Up in the Morning

We preachers are used to pushing aside the hectic chores of weekly pastoral work to ready a sermon for Sunday. Pressured by that countdown, we easily put the wrong question first. Students new to the preaching task and eager for success are no different. Students enter the semester wanting me to give them a method; they are asking me, "How do I preach?" And pastors, including me, too often take a look at Sunday's text and ask, "How am I going to preach *this?*"

"How?" is a question of technology and technique. It's not a wrong question; it's just the wrong question to ask first. It's a second question, and because of that it'll never be powerful enough to get preachers like you and me up in the morning. The first question, the big question, does have the power to get you up and keep you up. Ask

"Why?" and your pursuit of an answer will get you on your feet. Get moving on this question first, and the second question will follow well enough. So, when you get ready to preach, choose your questions carefully. Move out from inside the wrong question, put "How?" first, and you'll get sidetracked for longer than you can afford—or worse, you'll get derailed entirely.

Our preaching forms the world. Preaching is about using words in a daring act of creation. It's true that we preach good news, but preaching is more than that—preaching itself *is* good news. *Because* of preaching there is a future for the world. *Because* of preaching God has partners who speak the world into alignment with God, formed according to the kingdom, reordered, harmonized, whole, newborn. We don't dare underestimate the power of the words we utter. The Bible doesn't. "God spoke," Genesis tells us, and the world was created. The Bible testifies that when you and I preach we are uttering the grammar of life—the syntax of God's new world. And because of these words—offered even by the littlest of preachers, the most obscure handlers of the text, those who live and witness in places where they can only whisper a sermon—because of these words, daringly uttered, empires topple and God's new world is born.

Maybe that sounds audacious. And I'm sure it is. But it's the way I understand the work of the preacher. And there's nothing that can stand you on your feet again when anxiety bullies you and self-doubt sits on your chest and you can hardly breathe. No, there's nothing that'll stand you up again like believing *this* about the power of preaching, when you must stand beside a freshly dug grave and something whispers in your head, "Who are *you*? What do *you* think you have to offer these people?

Your little word-ritual is a sham, a masquerade, a whistling in the dark against forces more powerful than your little words." "How to preach?" isn't going to get you up to preach on the morning after a Saturday night when you've said rotten things to those you love, or on the Sunday after a meeting when key members of your church glare at you because of a controversial vote. In those moments, there's no technique in the world that can save you. In those times, unless you have at least some kind of answer to the first and big question, the littler "How?" simply won't get you going.

At those times when I'm weak and doubt overtakes me, when I feel I need another to stand with me as a witness to the Bible's own testimony to the power of the Word, I repeat to myself those little words of that gutsy dissident against the powers of death, Dietrich Bonhoeffer: "The truth shall set you free," he preached July 24, 1932. "Not our deed, not our courage or strength, not our people, not our truth, but God's truth alone. . . . [Those] who love, because they are freed through the truth of God, are the most revolutionary people on earth."

When I feel intimidated and insecure, foolish and powerless—at a graveside or beside a hospital bed, in the sanctuary or anywhere else—I remember that if there's just one person on earth who will speak that truth in freedom, then there's hope for the world. I imagine in that moment that I am that solitary person, and that's enough to get me through. It gets me up for one more day. If that's audacious, so be it.

A student once told me that all this sounds quite overwhelming—like some gigantic task the preacher must get up for. She worried that such a way of thinking about preaching could drop the weight and responsibility for the world and God's work heavy on our shoulders. For me, it works the opposite way. Freed from the "how" and into the "why" of preaching, I am free to live in the moment, with the sense of God with me and me with God. I am free to trust in the truth of God and therefore free to preach more humanly. To be me. To celebrate the creative Word. To utter these words with wild abandonment to their own power. To trust that my fragile words have a creative power that is not my own. All God asks is that I speak lovingly, daringly, and as truthfully as possible, dropping my masks, opening a vein, and bleeding. And when I do, there's not much burden in it at all.

Why it's not is beyond me, but it's a mystery I gladly embrace.

3

Truthfulness Will Set You Free

There are many influences on a preacher's life and ministry, and there are some persons and experiences that stand taller than others. For me, it's those who've not tried to teach me anything about preaching that have had the most enduring influence. Take the rock-and-roll band U2 for instance; I've probably learned as much about preaching from them and their lead singer, Bono, as I have from anyone else. I'm not alone in that—Karl Barth too sensed a kinship in a musician whose art bore witness to what he was trying to do theologically. About a section entitled "Nothingness" in *Church Dogmatics*, Barth once said: "I even let myself be carried away and devoted a special excursus to Mozart." He'd bought himself a gramophone, of which he wrote: "[It] virtually became a centerpiece at home, and a large number of Mozart records, which can often be heard in my study. Following a tendency that I had even as a small boy, I have now concentrated completely on Mozart and have established that in relation to him Bach is merely John the Baptist, and Beethoven, Origen, if not Shepherd of Hermas." About Barth's love for Mozart, his friend and biographer, Eberhard Busch wrote, "Barth's objection to Johann Sebastian Bach, otherwise so loved by theologians, was his all too deliberate, all too artificial 'desire to preach,' while Mozart attracted him because he was free from such intentions and simply played." It might be said of Mozart that he dropped his mask, opened a vein, and bled. I think that's exactly what Barth did with theology, and I think that's why he speaks so powerfully for preachers.

What Mozart did for Barth, U2's Bono does for me, and perhaps for other preachers as well—he frees me from "artificial desires to preach" and invites me to "simply play."

So many churches have no real room for the kind of honesty preaching requires. In fact, congregations and their preachers often move in a direction opposed to truthfulness and become places we experience as contrived, artificial environments where the raw stuff of real human life is kept out of bounds, despite the rawness of the texts we read together each week. This isn't just a problem for churches; it's part and parcel of the human condition, a condition torn open by poets who dare to tear things open, move beyond the artificial—the facade—and put their very skin on the table. Preaching at its best has been poetic; a kind of truth-telling—even if there are enormous pressures to do otherwise. Rock and roll, says Bono, isn't much different. There are enormous pressures to hide, deceive, and entertain, keeping us inside a false world. U2's success may just be at this point. They seem able to name pain in realistic and yet hopeful ways, to inhabit a song for the sake of the audience, drawing us all in, communicating all our humanness and vulnerability by the *way* they play for us as much as by what they say.

On September 1, 2001, for example, when U2 took the stage among 80,000 fans in the grassy amphitheater at Slane Castle in Ireland's County Meath, they did so in a place of rich and frightful Irish history. Here in the Boyne Valley megalithic tombs predate the pyramids. Nearby is Tara, the seat of Ireland's ancient high kings. Ireland's heroes, St. Patrick and Cuchuilain, are remembered for their exploits here, as is the 1680 battle that fueled the long-standing animosity between Irish Catholics and Protestants.

Right here, in early September 2001, with eerie prescience of a massive atrocity that would turn the world toward a long season of violence just ten days later, Bono and the band take aim at Irish violence. At the close of the song "Sunday, Bloody Sunday," a rant against the Omagh bombing that killed 29 people in a Northern Ireland market, Bono chants, one by one, the names of those killed and works to unmask the ideological gridlock behind not only this atrocity but every other atrocity like it.

This is rock and roll that cuts through masks and bleeds red the passion of the heart, saying to a world too often shrouded by lies that we are no longer willing to live inside your falsehoods. If rock and roll can do this, how much more must our preaching?

The 2005 book *Bono* (a series of conversations between the editor, Michka Assayas, and Bono of U2) gives us a window on the singer and truly great soul meditating on the way of such truthfulness. The conversation invites us to consider ways we preachers might learn from U2. In what follows I take some license with Assayas's conversation with Bono in order to tilt the conversation toward the work we preachers do.

> *Bono*: Rather than putting your skin on the table, [so much rock and roll is about] finding a second skin, a mask.
>
> *Erdman*: The same is true in our churches. Folks wear their masks, put on the thick skin. And it's the preachers who train us all in this false world. We hide. We perform. Our fears keep us from the true work you call us to . . . exposing our hearts, putting our bodies on the line, bleeding for the gospel.
>
> *Michka*: Bono, how do you reconcile your earnestness with the need for a showbiz facade?
>
> *Erdman*: And how can preachers run hard and away from the Sirens who invite us toward the showbiz facade that's so terribly alluring? There's not one of us who isn't tempted to try to "wow" the masses. And by the simplest of measures, facade appears to work.
>
> *Bono*: Never trust a performer, performers are the best liars. They lie for a living. . . . You're an actor, in a certain sense. But a writer is not a liar. There's a piece of Scripture: "Know the truth, and the truth will set you free." Even as a child, I remember sitting, listening to my teacher in school talking about the great Irish poet William Butler Yeats. He had writer's block—there was a period where he couldn't write. I put my hand up and said: "Why didn't

he write about that?"—"Don't be stupid. Put your hand down, don't be so cheeky." But I didn't mean it as a smart-arse. I have lived off that idea: "Know the truth, the truth will set you free." If I've nothing to say, that's the first line of the song.

In fact, even on our second album [October], I [sang] about having nothing to say: "I try to sing this song . . . I try to stand up but I can't find my feet / I try to speak up but only with you am I complete." This has always been the trick for me. And maybe it is just that: a trick. But it tricks me out of myself. I am able to write, always, because as a writer, I am always unable not to be true. As a performer, it isn't always so.

You know the thing that keeps me honest as a performer? The f–king high notes I have to sing. Because unless I am totally in that character, I actually can't sing—it's out of my range. That's what keeps me honest on a stage.

Erdman: Oh, for preachers who would dare to sing high notes, and find a way to fling themselves out into that kind of honesty. If so, we might be able to call what we do "preaching."

4

Toward a New (Old) Way of Preaching

Preaching for me invariably falls flat, is too much work, and fails to be honest and free when I am too self-conscious—when I'm worried and anxious about the task of preparing the text and hosting it among the people, when I'm worried and anxious about how I am doing and if I'm right enough or good enough or relevant enough. After many years at it and among various congregations, preaching is at its best in me precisely when I am *least* self-conscious, when I am absorbed in the moment, when I care as little as I possibly can about how I'm coming across to the congregation, when I am engaged, present, absorbed in or actually inhabiting the text as if lost in rapt attentiveness and adoration.

"How" is not the first question we bring to the preaching task, but it is still a question, and it may now be time to open it up. There is a journey toward this place of being fully present and true before the text, present and true before the congregation, God, myself.

There was a time when I used to work so hard on my sermons during the week that I'd get myself stuck some-where along the way and in frustration and anxiety end up throwing a commentary across the room because the whole thing seemed to be coming apart before my very eyes. I'd write and write. I'd look for just the right illus-tration. I'd get in the sanctuary and try to imagine my people. And come Saturday night, I'd be so uptight that I was frankly no fun to be around—*every* week. Weekends were a drag for my family because I was a preacher. But finally, after long years, I came to a point of crisis when I realized not only that this grinding away at the text felt like it was all wrong, but also that I could not be a preacher this way and be a husband and father—or a human being, for that matter—much longer.

During that time, it was one of my weekly practices to go out, usually Wednesdays, and serve Communion to shut-ins. An elderly man—one of our church elders—would go with me. He'd lived a long time and heard a lot of sermons. He knew the Bible front and back, and so our habit was to allow him to choose a short Bible text for us to read among the shut-ins that day prior to Commu-nion. For instance, as we'd drive to the first house I'd say something like, "Dick, what do you think our shut-ins need to hear from God today?" Dick would sift through his brain and come out with a text. I'd say, "That sounds good. Will you read it and offer prayer when we get to that point in our visit? Then I'll say a few things about it before we break the bread."

After several months of this, Dick said to me, "You know, Pastor, you preach better to our shut-ins than you do to us on Sundays. I don't mean that the way it might sound. It's a compliment. I've heard a lot of sermons. Some very good. But what I think we need most is for the preacher to get away from the notes, look us in the eye and help us see."

Serving Communion with Dick Long was just what I needed during that crisis in my life—as a preacher and as a husband and father. Dick's witness and challenge changed my life. It may have saved my marriage. It certainly has made it so that I can enjoy being a pastor and preacher. Maybe in the long run, it's saved my life. I certainly sleep better on Saturday nights. And I haven't thrown a commentary in nearly a decade. What I love most is that my wife will sometimes ask me on Saturday night who's preaching the next day. And when I say, "I am," I realize how far I've come. In the past, before I learned what is for me a new (but probably very old) way to preach, she always knew exactly who was preaching the next day. And it wasn't anticipation for the Word of God that excited her.

5

Preaching on the Run—
Toward a Simpler Way to Prepare

I've moved a long way over time from the uptight, rule-bound exegetical process and sermon-writing method that I thought was the right way to prepare. I must confess that it's not necessarily the fault of those who trained me, though few of them really helped. I'm a recovering perfectionist, and I grew up feeling that I could never be right enough or do things well enough. "If a job's worth doing, it's worth doing right." That was ingrained within me at an early age. But over time there've been some subtle and not so subtle challenges to that phrase that had damned me to live inside a cramped little world even as I pursued the freedom of the gospel.

There was a moment during my master's work in seminary when a British professor, Colin Brown, was introducing a rather daunting syllabus to us and we were feeling quite overwhelmed. My stomach was knotting up inside me at the load of work and because of my drive to do it all and do it all well. At one point, he must have sensed our angst. He leaned over the lectern, peered over his glasses at us and said, "If a job's worth doing . . ." And I thought to myself, "Here it comes again." But instead, Brown said, "If a job's worth doing, it's worth doing poorly. Just do it!" Crack—something broke inside me. Nothing big. But the world I'd been living in for so long began to crumble. It didn't crumble without a fight. But God's mischief kept coming at me in so many ways—some terribly painful, others simply "aha's."

Another moment came years later, when, during my doctoral work, another professor took a whack at what was left of that perfectionist world. Walter Brueggemann, teaching Jeremiah to a handful of us preachers, said something like, "I know what you pastors must do week in and week out; well, here's a little exegetical method for preaching on the run" (more on this in chapter 7). I grabbed onto that phrase, "preaching on the run." That's exactly how I lived my weeks. Pastoral work was messy. And no matter how much I still tried (even as a recovering perfectionist) to control it, my weeks belied every effort to keep pastoral work manageable and carve out my needed twenty hours a week in sermon preparation.

I'd learned somewhere along the way that a good pastor spent mornings in exegesis and study, and afternoons in calling and other administrative tasks. And a good pastor could not possibly preach on Sundays without spending at least twenty hours in this work—solid exegesis and the writing of a quality sermon. Well, that wasn't my life, no matter how much I tried to live up to it and no matter how I chastened myself for my failures. Maybe this just makes public my neuroses, but I've a sense that there are a whole lot of others who live under this kind of tyranny. And that's true not just for mainline preachers, but for those who are bullied by the requirements of Fundamentalist certitude as well as those wowed by the communication excellence of the nation's megachurch superstars.

"If a job's worth doing, it's worth doing poorly. Just do it." Colin Brown's words spoke to me of something real, a preacher's discipleship for those weeks when a family in crisis, a staff conflict, and a weekend wedding all mean I can't do what I once thought I had to do during the week to be a good preacher. "A little exegetical method for preachers on the run." Walter Brueggemann's words describe my life and, I think, are much more consistent with the way I read the Bible's way of describing the preaching task. With prophets and apostles and Jesus too, it's always done on the run.

Preaching is something lived. It comes out of who we are. Our task is simply to stay close to the text, stay close to who we are as witnesses to Jesus Christ (in all of our unique and God-breathed mystery and strength and necessity), and stay close to our people among whom we're sent to host this text week in and week out. I can do that on the run. And if I do, it's always good. I've come to believe that maybe it's good precisely because my sermon *won't* be printed in a book or recorded on a CD or made available for digital download.

Now when my students ask, "How long does your sermon preparation take?" I answer, "A lifetime. No less, no more."

Incidentally, this isn't what I have learned on my own. In my community we are learning this together. In this congregation, we all (pastors and lay preachers alike) are finding this a way much more consistent with who we are and how we understand the task of hosting the biblical text among God's people whenever we gather. It's a way of preaching we can *all* practice.

Monday
A Prayer before the Word

On 1 John 5:9–13
Seventh Sunday of Easter, 2003

You, God—
who have uttered your testimony,
    a testimony that risks misunderstanding and
      ridicule,
    a testimony made vulnerable to the devices of the
      powerful,
    a testimony offered in relentless faithfulness,
    a testimony given in confidence that it will
      conquer the world,
    a testimony received in unrestrained joy.

We come to you—
who calls us to receive and believe your testimony
even when human opinions make more sense,
    when human politics seem more capable,
    when human technology seems more competent,
    when human desires seem more compelling.

We come to you and this text of yours—
you urge us to trust that your words are greater,
    more trustworthy,
    more lasting,
    more desirable,
    more transforming than anything we humans
      have to offer.

Come among us,
and help us believe your testimony,
and by believing
to live in the joyous freedom of the children of God,
who know the eternal life given us and the world in
    your Son,
Jesus Christ,
who sends us from this place
to testify on his behalf.

Amen.

6

Choosing Texts—The Lectionary, the Christian Year, and Forming an Alternative People

I began my Christian journey as a young adult in congregations that ostensibly put a high premium on the Bible in worship. We let the preacher choose whatever text he thought we needed to hear each week, usually linked to the preacher's sermon series that addressed the felt needs of the congregation. Looking back over time, I realized that the sermon and the text (oftentimes read somewhere in the middle of the preacher's sermon) were more launching pads for the pastor's personal self-interest or agenda for us than an entrance for the people of God into the wondrous and often strange world of the Bible—that odd text that wants to perform its own mischief among us beyond whatever the preacher wants to do to us.

To avoid this, early in my own ministry I began to preach through books of the Bible. I was trying to avoid the pitfalls of a felt-needs preaching regimen, but this strategy wasn't without problems. As I journeyed through the years with my congregation, I began to realize that the rhythms of the calendar had a profound effect on our lives and in many ways pressured my preaching. The first day of school, Thanksgiving, Christmas, New Year's Day, the Super Bowl, spring break, Easter, Mother's Day, Veterans' Day, Memorial Day, the Fourth of July, Labor Day all made claims on the congregation. And I found it difficult to plan a year's series of sermons on books of the Bible that worked, given the powerful presence of the calendar that gave shape to our lives. It was during this same time that I began sensing an even deeper conflict between this calendar and the seasons of the Christian year that were trying to get our attention.

I voiced my consternation to my friend Ed Searcy, who set me on a path that's revolutionized my preaching and immersed our congregation in a peculiarly Christian way of marking the seasons of the year. He said, "You're working too hard. For millennia, the church has lived under the text of scripture in ways that keep it hearing the gospel season after season and forming the life of congregations as a missional people. Try preaching the lectionary—it gives you as preacher the gift of freedom that comes from *not* having to choose your own text each week; it also gives your people the gift of the Christian year. The Christian year's annual retelling and reliving of the story of the gospel is a powerful teaching resource for churches and disciples who live in cultures that have forgotten, or have never heard, the Christian story."

In our congregation, we've been preaching the lectionary ever since and learning that the church consciously does *not* follow the calendar year, the school year, the commercial year . . . *primarily*, that is. We also know that as disciples we must responsibly live inside the way the rest of the world marks time. Conscious of those ways of practicing time, we practice reading from the Revised Common Lectionary's selection of Bible texts each Sunday; they keep us anchored to a particularly and peculiarly Christian way of keeping time.

Our people struggled with this approach at first—it felt terribly foreign to us all (so deeply were we formed by a non-Christian practice of time). But after seven years our people will tell you that there is a genuine biblical renewal among us. Last year, the congregation wrote their own Advent devotional—there wasn't an ounce of *Chicken Soup for the Soul* in it; each person, teenagers included, lived under the text, allowing it to form their meditations and lead us into a fuller embrace of the evangelical hope of Advent, which was more robust than any of us had ever experienced before.

We're finding that there is something deeply consistent with discipleship when we can't choose the words we will hear each Sunday, the texts our preachers read and ponder among us. And I think this moves the right direction on the interpretive bridge. Our people now want our preachers to host the text in all its strangeness, standing with them beneath it, even (maybe especially) when it is beguiling and confusing, dark and troubling. And their desires now square with my own—I'm not much interested in moving from the world we live in toward the text and trying to square its old ways with this new world as if the text must be made relevant to us. Rather, I think the text

43

wants to make *us* relevant to God. And the text—not our own agendas, opinions, or desires—is the birthplace of God's new life for us and for the world.

Here I betray my philosophical and epistemological biases. The world is texted. We are all scripted. The world is formed by the power of speech; I mean that quite literally. Without words, texts, stories there is nothing. Perhaps there is some "foundation" behind all the words, but frankly that "foundation" is a wisp and a dream. We can't access any "foundation" behind reality, even if it does exist. All we have is words, and so I take words and the words I, as preacher, host among our people very, very seriously. And I think this is precisely what the Bible and those who've long cherished it mean to do.

With this as background, here's how we generally practice using the lectionary:

The person hosting the text (the preacher) among us will choose from any of the four texts (one each from the Old Testament, the Psalms, the Gospels, and a New Testament epistle), though we have found that we may linger for a season in one particular stream of the readings. For example, we've spent the last few summers in the Old Testament readings. One fall, we read the Psalms and explored what it means to learn to pray by praying the Psalms and letting them form our speech toward God. In Advent we walked among the prophets. In Lent we were engaged by the Gospels. During this last Easter and Pentecost we weaved in and out among the Acts of the Apostles and the Gospel of John. Among our children (the children's sermon) we may read a smaller portion of one of the four readings—attending to its formative power with the same deliberativeness as we choose the reading for the day's sermon. Often, we will use the Psalm text for the day as a reading, meditation, or prayer. All this is true not only for our traditional but also for our contemporary service. And even our alternative or postmodern evening service is entering the future by digging into the past—tutored by the older ways.

Sundays are not the only place the lectionary is forming our life. In committee meetings our elders read one of the upcoming Sunday texts, and our *lectio divina* groups do the same. People, no longer living inside the insidious individualism that has too long formed our lives, don't have to choose a devotional text that speaks to our needs in the moment. They are invigorated by letting the text surprise them and speak them toward its own relevance—which doesn't always make them feel good, but almost always gives them a sense of being disturbed toward God and formed as a people who can live by a story that counters the stories and other verbiage that passes for life in a world captive to death in all its disguises.

7

Thirty to Sixty Minutes
Each Monday

For preachers on the run, exegesis can hover around three simple steps: a close reading of the text, a study of key words, and discerning the text's agenda. These are the basics Walter Brueggemann taught me—he offers a handy little guide to these three steps in the introduction of his Jeremiah commentary. I heartily recommend those few pages. They're the most helpful bit of exegetical advice I've come across. The helpfulness of those few pages comes not only from their brevity, but from Walter's life as he's immersed himself in the text and among pastors and their congregations for a long, long time.

On Mondays, after I've identified the text or texts for the coming Sunday, I take my Bible and photocopy the text, then cut out the pericope so that I can run a legal-size sheet of paper through the copier and have just this text on a single page—with plenty of white space around it for scribbling notes and observations and questions (it's the questions that probably help me most—they energize my inquiry). I don't remember much of the Greek and Hebrew I once learned, so I'm working strictly with English. That doesn't intimidate me. It'd be nice to be able to work with the biblical languages, and those who can do so with ease probably have some kind of advantage. But I feel quite confident when working with what tools I've been given. Don't you ever feel like a second-class citizen for not knowing the languages, and frankly, if you're not good with them, I wouldn't take the time to become proficient. Pastoral ministry requires too much to be saddled with that on top of everything else; you're a pastor, not an academic. And you *are* a theologian. But most of your theological work will be done on the run.

So, after I've got the text on a sheet of paper in front of me, I'll take thirty to sixty minutes (usually in the late morning) to read the text as closely as possible. That means that I'm paying very careful attention to how the text is put—that is, I'm doing rhetorical analysis of the text. The books most helpful for me in this regard have been Phyllis Trible's book *Rhetorical Criticism* and Ken Bailey's *Poet and Peasant* and *Through Peasant Eyes*. Both scholars will model for you ways to evaluate the clues of meaning in the text itself. You're looking for word repetition, parallelism, chiasm—things like these. Sometimes it's tough to see the forest for the trees, but persisting for an hour in this kind of close reading can yield wonderful results—you begin to see the relationships of words and, of course, their connection to the material around your sermon text.

Here's an example: I was getting ready to preach on 1 Samuel 4 recently—the story of Israel's defeat by the

Philistines, and the capture of the ark—and my close reading of the text made me aware of the marvelous turn in the text from the world plunged into chaos by men with big names and big wars to fight, but who, for all their machinery, could not keep the nation from a national security crisis. The text shows all those things, but then it turns on the little phrase, "Now his daughter-in-law." In this little phrase, artfully tendered, I saw the theologians of exile who cherished this text tipping their hat through this rhetorical turn. Around this phrase the narrative turns from the international crisis involving men, politics, and war, toward the smaller, deeper, and pregnant-with-meaning story of interpersonal despair and astonishing hope. Arising from this text are the unnamed women, the midwives of history who cradle God's newness—our future—in their hands and whisper the Word of God: "Do not be afraid, you have borne a son." It wasn't hard to glimpse where this might take us. Just sixty minutes and I'd hit pay dirt.

That's Monday. I simply get into the text by looking at its rhetoric. And you can do that with a good English Bible as well as with the Greek or Hebrew if you have it. But I tell my students, don't fret too much about trying to unlock the secrets. Just get into it for as much time as you've got. And go with what you see. Then close your Bible, put what you've started to learn in your little file folder, and go on with your other ministry tasks. You'll come back to it for another brief dip tomorrow and carry things deeper still.

8

Let the Stories Crawl Out All by Themselves

When you preach you must never tame the text. There's been too much of that. These sacred texts that bear the Word of God are anything but tame. The Bible, and the Character whose story it tells in such a wide and wild variety of ways, just can't be tamed or flattened or simplified or reduced or distilled into some bland tonic or a handful of nifty words that the listener, eager pen in hand, can stuff into blanks on some silly sermon note-taking sheet. No, when you preach you must respect this text more than that, and give it and its Author full room to do their own work.

If you want to know how to handle this text, I'll steer you toward the novelist John Steinbeck over the mass of contemporary preachers. Steinbeck knows how to handle the kind of stories, rants, poems, prayers, commands, and whatever else makes up the pages of the Bible. Steinbeck knows nature and the human condition into which you and I are sent to preach the gospel. Here's Steinbeck with a pretty accurate description of the preacher's art—

> Cannery Row in Monterey in California is a poem, a stink, a grating noise, a quality of light, a tone, a habit, a nostalgia, a dream. . . . How can the poem and the stink and the grating noise—the quality of light, the tone, the habit and the dream—be set down alive? When you collect marine animals there are certain flat worms so delicate that they are almost impossible to capture whole, for they break and tatter under the touch. You must let them ooze and crawl of their own will onto the knife blade and then lift them gently into your bottle of sea water. And perhaps that might be the way to write this book—to open the page and to let the stories crawl in by themselves.

I'm hard-pressed to imagine a better way of handling the Bible . . . and opening its pages among those whose lives are as full of as much stink and noise, light, tone, and habit as those whose lives the Bible wants us to capture whole. Work too hard at getting them out and off the page, and you'll do them damage or injustice. Better to open the page and let the stories crawl out all by themselves. That's when your preaching will be its best, and you'll find yourself working at your task with more wonder and a lot less chore.

9

How to Be Good (at Preaching)

The best way to be a really good preacher is by not trying to be good at all. If you're going to be good, you must put being good out of your mind. Trying to be good has at best produced some silly caricatures of preaching. At worst, trying to be good is an alluring Siren that has caused many a preacher to crash on the rocks of ambition. You are not sent by the Lord Jesus to be good. That said, I've no doubt that you can be good so long as being good is not your aim.

I can remember an embarrassing but healing moment during my first days in seminary. It happened over twenty years ago, but it's still vivid in my mind. Proud of the sermon I'd preached the Sunday before leaving home and moving to Fuller Seminary in the Los Angeles area, and still warmed by the accolades of those who loved me, I carried a tape of that sermon, intent on giving it to a preaching professor upon my arrival. Within days of stepping onto campus, I did what I'd determined to do—I'd set up a meeting with a preaching professor and, after some light conversation, handed him the tape, essentially saying, "Listen to this and preview the extraordinary gifts of a student you'll soon get to work with." I'm sure it didn't come across that brash or stupid, but looking back after all these years that's exactly what it was. The professor was generous and, having faced the pride of many young preachers, disarmed my arrogance with grace and wit. Handing the tape back to me, he told me he was eager to hear me preach and that the day would come soon enough. He didn't say so then but could have: ambition and arrogance are qualities that preachers must crucify, not nurture.

Some of the students who come into my preaching classes are as arrogant as I once was; they think they're already quite good and that I'm lucky to have them. Others want to be good and think they're paying me to show them how. Some are just plain terrified—while they feel some compulsion to preach, it scares the daylights out of them and they're not sure they'll ever be good enough. It's the last group of preachers who will learn to preach. And unless those in the other two groups learn to lose their pride, they'll find themselves popular speakers, perhaps even growing large institutions, but they'll never be preachers of the gospel, forming congregations of disciples.

Here's why trying to be good or thinking you are good is no good for the preacher. When you're trying to be good, you spin off mental and spiritual energy that you need to rightly handle the Word. You split your energies between preaching the Word and evaluating how you're doing at preaching. When you're preaching you must inhabit the moment as fully as possible. You cannot afford to split yourself. When you do, something becomes false, rings hollow. We've all seen preachers who can't hide the sense we have about them that inside they're saying, "Okay, now I make this gesture . . . now walk left . . . smile broadly . . . oh look, they really liked that." There is a self-consciousness that wanting to be good brings into the preaching moment that has no business there at all. Self-consciousness creates an anxiety to impress that most of us can sniff out a mile away.

When you try to be good, you are not good. You may be good in that veneer sense of being good that tricks only the undiscerning, but your drive to be good means that your gifts and personhood (which are part and parcel of the way God wills to reveal the Word in our world) get all gummed up—they can't work well at all because you are constantly worrying and evaluating and fretting, instead of living free, released to live in this moment, just this moment, asking only, "Lord, what's coming to me now, right now?"

Brenda Ueland in her marvelous little book *If You Want to Write: A Book about Art, Independence, and Spirit* (a required text in my preaching classes) says, "I know a fine concert pianist who says sadly of a terribly hard-working but hopeless pupil: 'She always practices and never plays.'" Wanting to be good gums up her natural giftedness, which must be released to do what it can do quite well if given the chance and not bullied around by an overweening desire to be good, impress people, and stand head and shoulders above the rest.

To be good, you must live in the present. That means there is no trafficking back and forth between what you are doing and how you're doing at it. Bad preachers, those who are sad caricatures of the real thing, are those who are "always practicing and never playing"—they've never learned to fling themselves out into the wonder, freedom, and necessity of their own God-breathed originality.

Get inside that, and you'll be good. Better yet, preach from inside that place, and you'll never have to worry about whether you are good or not. You simply are, and that's a goodness God can work with.

10

Preaching as an Alternative to Violence

Human history is a long and sordid history of violence. We preachers have been preaching for a good many of those years. Given the fact that Jesus came into a violent world preaching, rejecting the military option, and armed only with the Word, and whose witness in the face of violence actually breaks the back of violence, it's strange to me how our preaching has too often formed congregations that are essentially acolytes to state-sanctioned violence rather than an alternative and a challenge to it.

The Bible speaks of a day when wars will cease, when we "shall beat [our] swords into ploughshares, and [our] spears into pruning hooks; nation shall not lift up sword against nation, neither shall they learn war any more" (Isaiah 2:4). The way we preachers preach and the way our preaching forms congregations ought to witness that this day has come among us in Jesus Christ.

The only weapon Jesus used was the Word. The only weapon the church is to use is the Word (Ephesians 6:17). We are told that the "weapons of our warfare are not merely human, but they have divine power" (2 Corinthians 10:4). We are told that through death Jesus destroyed "the one who has the power of death, that is, the devil, and free[d] those who all their lives were held in slavery by their fear of death" (Hebrews 2:14–15). And we have the whole of the Revelation to John as a sustained testimony of the church's understanding that Jesus has changed everything and is changing everything. It witnesses to the fact that the first Christians realized that just as Jesus's preaching was *the* power above all powers, so too the word of their testimony, their *preaching,* had the power to undo and redo the whole world. It was a word that could make the empires of the world tremble. It was a word that would shake the empires to their core and topple their arrogant usurpation of God's authority. They knew that following Jesus meant that they would conquer the world for God not militarily, but *homiletically*—"they conquered [the Violent One] by the blood of the Lamb and by the word of their testimony, for they did not cling to life even in the face of death" (Revelation 12:11).

Aleksandr Solzhenitsyn in our time knew this. In his 1970 acceptance speech for the Nobel Prize in literature he said—and it ought to be seriously reconsidered in our age so rife with falsehoods that promote violence, war, and destruction—

> And the simple step of a simple courageous man is not to partake in falsehood, not to support false actions! Let *that* enter the world, let it even reign in the world—but not with

my help. But writers and artists can achieve more: they can *conquer falsehood!* In the struggle with falsehood art always did win and it always does win! Openly, irrefutably for everyone! Falsehood can hold out against much in this world, but not against art. And no sooner will falsehood be dispersed than the nakedness of violence will be revealed in all its ugliness—and violence, decrepit, will fall.

That is why, my friends, I believe that we are able to help the world in its white-hot hour. Not by making the excuse of possessing no weapons, and not by giving ourselves over to a frivolous life—but by going to war!

One word of truth shall outweigh the whole world!

The church possesses "weapons" that hold a power the world cannot fathom. The first Christians (and there have been many since) knew that this word of truth spoken in the name of Jesus might well cost them their lives. But they were unwilling to consider safety the key issue. So long as violence holds sway in the world, no one is safe. Life is precarious.

Many today condemn nonviolence as a non-strategy, as a utopian ideal. Nonviolence will mean certain death in the face of violent powers. But what do we trust more to protect us and make this world safe? Our bombs or the word of Jesus Christ? There is no evidence at all that violence, even just violence, makes us safer. But there is ample evidence that it only keeps us captive to the long and sordid history of violence that is ours in this world.

Christian preaching was meant to be an alternative to violence. Jesus *is* God's alternative to violence . . . and the church is to be his disciple. Some will say that all this isn't what preaching is for. We say this only because real preaching hasn't been dared. We say this only because our reliance on violence and our practice of offering our preaching in service to the state is a witness to our evangelical loss of nerve, that we really don't believe in the power of the Word of God.

What the world needs, at this our "white-hot hour," is our testimony. And toward this end, I'd recast Solzhenitsyn's words to writers so that they speak their truth to us preachers: "In the struggle with falsehood *preaching* always did win and it always does win! Openly, irrefutably for everyone! Falsehood can hold out against much in this world, but not against *preaching.*"

Jesus came not with a sword, but with *words*; he conquered the world nonviolently. He came *preaching*—exposing the falsehood of this world. *If* we follow him, "the nakedness of violence will be revealed in all its ugliness—and violence, decrepit, will fall."

And we preachers, with our preaching congregations, will lead the world in its true exodus.

Tuesday

A Prayer before the Word

On Philippians 4:1–9
October 9, 2005

You chose to use words to create the world,
flimsy nouns and verbs and adjectives and tiny
    articles;
and you choose to use words to recreate the world,
spoken by persons
sometimes weak and frightened,
other times strong and daring . . .
all times vulnerable to forces that seem so much
    mightier than these words of ours,
forces that would shut us up and shut us down . . .
as they did the living Word;
the Word made flesh;
the Word crucified;
the Word locked away and ignored . . .
until Sunday.

Now, and every Sunday since—
we rise in joy to feed on nouns and verbs and adjec-
    tives and tiny articles.
For we know that no one lives by bread alone,
but by all those words that proceed from your
    mouth,
and now from ours.
So, feed us again,
and we will be the people on this earth

who know the language of heaven—
that language from which a whole new world is
    born.
And we, if we choose our words with care, help bring
    it into being.

Amen.

11

On Tuesdays I Chase Words

When Tuesdays come, I chase down words like a tomcat chasing mice. From the Monday task of looking at the larger arrangement of those words—repetition, shifts in scene or voice, comparisons, metaphors, contrasts, and other rhetorical clues that can render surprises not apparent at first glance—I move to the Tuesday task of looking at the words themselves. I'm arguing (and others have argued this better than I can) that *what* the text means is in large measure dependent on *how* it is said.

On Tuesdays (if I'm lucky enough to be able to keep the weekly discipline from unraveling up to this point), I'll take another hour to jot down the words or short phrases that my Monday work suggests are significant. On Monday I copied the Sunday text on a piece of legal-sized paper with plenty of white space around the text for notes, observations, and questions. I also began underlining repetitions, circling key words or phrases, scribbling references to other scripture texts that I think might have bearing on this one. On Tuesdays, I create a short list of words or phrases that merit further study. For example, "witness" in John 1:7 not only often appears in the Johannine literature but also in Isaiah. I'd like to chase down those other references and see how John uses the word and then learn if there's any hint that his use is influenced by Isaiah. My study of 1 Samuel 4, for example, meant that I chased down words like "Ichabod" and the sense of Yahweh's departure, not only in the following chapters of Yahweh's exile in Ashdod, but also the "glory's" departure in Ezekiel—an exilic prophet sympathetic to the Samuel material in front of me. I also chased after the word "midwives," and nearly chased it all over the Bible. Then there was "do not be afraid," and I could hardly catch my breath at the breadth of references. Add to this the "you have borne a son" and its variants and I finally stood breathless, enrapt before the Word.

I confess that I'm not always good at chasing these words. Sometimes I'm just not feeling inquisitive enough. At other times, I'm rushed and have to operate on my best hunch or instinct. But after years in the text, that's not such a bad wager—though I'd not want to do always what I can sometimes do well enough.

Of course, if you're well versed in the languages, your study may yield more fruit than does the study of those of us who don't share your gifts. But even those of us working only in English (or some other language) can make good enough use of Bible dictionaries and commentaries and will glean something helpful. I remind you, here's a task that could consume many, many hours. Most of us just don't have that kind of time. So, set yourself a time limit. If you've got two hours, enjoy the gift. If all you've got for this Tuesday task is a quarter of that, don't kick yourself. Chase away and carry with you what mice you may.

12

On Crossing the Line— The Public Preaching of Our Private Darkness

I'm teaching technique in these pages, to be sure, but technique must not obscure what is the more important task—exploring the person of the preacher. The book began with an appeal for preachers to preach as authentically and vulnerably as they can. "Drop your masks, open a vein, and bleed for God," I wrote in the first chapter. If you've come along with me this far and if you've stepped into any of this in your own ministry, you'll probably voice what one colleague did when she heard me say such a thing. "In my experience in congregations, my vulnerability and authenticity cannot go into the realm of doubts that challenge group norms about truth, or gospel, or biblical inspiration. Cross these norms, and you'll have prompt and concerned, even scandalized reactions."

She puts her finger on something many who are reading this book may themselves be feeling. It's one thing to express your own foibles, personal dilemmas, and humanness to the people to whom you belong as their preacher. It is another thing to express your doubts, your flirtations with heresy, your downright anger at God, your distaste for parts of the Bible that make your head spin. The truth is, many of us dare not go into these places—at least consciously. We admit our brokenness in human relationships—trouble with our kids or spouse, with our bodies. And most of our people will go along with us if we enter these places publicly (though not all will; even these vulnerabilities can deeply threaten some). Most of us know that people can be helped pastorally when they realize that even their pastors struggle with the things they face. Most of us can go here. But there are many of us who don't or won't allow ourselves to doubt, to fight with God, rage at God, disapprove of God's ways or words. There are lines we are as afraid to cross as our people are. And frankly, we're greatly responsible for their unwillingness to do so.

There are at least two related things that are necessary if we are to truly "open a vein and bleed for God," and do it publicly.

First, we need time—gobs of time—with a people, so that we can grow in our ability to cross the line (and for *them* to grow into their ability to let us). When I first started dating my wife, Julie, I drew the line much farther outside myself than I do today. There are places she can cross over into my life now that I would never have dreamed of allowing then, when trust was much more fragile.

Second, time—long seasons of it—is also necessary for me to learn about me. When I feel unsafe, there are places I simply will not go. I think that's true with the kind of doubts and frustrations and tendency toward heresy that most of us deny. Until we've journeyed with ourselves long enough, we simply don't know they are there. And if we're not in relationships with others who can give us safe places to express these things, they will lie buried—troubling us in so many other, subtle ways we're not aware of.

Our churches are places where we stuff these things because we all are terribly fragmented and have such precious little time with each other. Pastors who are among a people for a very long time are able to build the kind of relationships with their people out of which there can be the expression of these frightening and disturbing things (things I think are very important and helpful to the life of the disciple-community). And it is out of this durable, time-matured relationship that such expressions become helpful. I do think that too much line-crossing too early or too quickly is unhelpful and dangerous.

What we're talking about is an art, not a science. An amateur sculptor can ruin a good piece of marble with the same chisel a master uses to make a masterpiece. A would-be brain surgeon can kill a patient lickety-split, while a master surgeon can bring a whole new chapter in a person's life. Stupid pastors, unaware of the effect of their bewilderment, pain, or arrogance—pastors who are selfish and narcissistic—can do a lot of damage, while saints can put things in just the right way, preaching their darkness, "opening a vein" in such a way that folks are saved and made saints themselves, precisely because of their darkness.

13

Do Preachers Really Have This Freedom?

It's one thing to say these things; it's another thing to do them, or to be able to do them. Kristin Fast, a thoughtful friend and exceptional writer and poet, heard me saying the kinds of things I said earlier about U2 and the preaching task, and wrote of her concerns—concerns that name what many of us preachers feel:

> It seems like preachers are in a difficult spot when it comes to being honest in the way you offer U2's Bono as a model for preachers. Do preachers really have the freedom to stand before the people and say, "You know what? I'm having trouble believing this stuff lately," or "God seems really silent and distant these days," or "I've worked and prayed and meditated in order to have something to say, and I've really come up dry this week"? The pressure and responsibil-

ity seem great to be a beacon of faith and inspiration and hard driving advocacy for the gospel when sometimes the raw stuff in our souls isn't anywhere close to those things. Honesty and truth and our humanity seem to create a real quandary for preachers.

Kristin puts her finger on a real dilemma we preachers face. And I resonate with it—I often feel the temptation to hide, to put on a show, to lie about myself, and by doing so perpetuate the lies we all carry around with us as God's church. But I live and preach among a people who are teaching me as much as I am teaching them. And the longer we are together, the more permission we have to enter the real human condition that the gospel invites us to embrace. U2 was able to say the things they said about the IRA and Irish politics in that potent geography at Slane Castle because Ireland is their home; the Irish are their tribe, and U2 is Ireland's band. To move toward honesty, real "reach beneath your ribs and pull" honesty, requires presence among a people, the durability of relationship. And it is just what we pastors ought to have as those who are commissioned by our people to host their terribly honest texts week in and week out.

Because of the length of relationship—my life lived among their lives over years of ministry—I felt quite comfortable "opening my ribcage" or "putting my skin on the table" recently. Well, *comfortable* may not be the right word—*able* or *free* or maybe even *compelled* are more accurate. I limped through the first part of a particular worship service holding tremendous emotional pain inside me, wanting to wear a mask but feeling the increasing burden and falsehood of doing so. When the time came to preach, I realized that I couldn't hide my pain and really preach, so I began my sermon this way:

In one way I'm not fit to preach today. Last night I was a real jerk to my sons. Said things that hurt and cut deeply. Things I regret. Things no father should say. I feel like a hypocrite today, and frankly I'm a little bitter that I have to be a preacher. I feel like maybe it's not fair being a preacher who has to be human, do stupid things, then have to open the Bible before you all the next morning and act like I've got it together. Fortunately, you give me permission to be human and to say that I'm not fit today. And my hunch is that I'm not alone in this. Maybe we're all not fit in one way or another.

So, I'll tell you what I'm going to do. I'm going to open this text among you because I need it as much or more than anybody else. And maybe as I open this text out of my own desperate need you will join me. I've a hunch that we all in one way or another need what this text offers us today. None of us is fit enough to preach if being fit means being all put together. Maybe it's the recognition that being "not put together" is exactly what makes us fit to host this text that means life and hope and salvation for us and the world.

That's what I said and that's what my community allows, permits, and in increasing measure demands—even though I don't "bleed" in this personal way with regularity. Such regular personal openness would end up a silly and abusive use of my role and personhood and family. On that Sunday morning, I was afraid to say these things publicly, not so much because folks wouldn't allow it, but because I feared my "bleeding" would obscure the text. Later, people expressed to me that my confession actually freed them from the masks they bring into the room and gave them permission to be human and to bring that humanness to the text rather than to hide it from the text. This is precisely what preaching ought to do.

There are quandaries of course, as Kristin notes, but fortunately I rarely feel them now. Perhaps that's because of the kind of people among whom I've lived for quite a while, the kind of people we're becoming, and perhaps because of the kind of person and preacher they are making me to be.

I must add that "opening a vein and bleeding for God" is not first of all about personal vulnerability in the therapeutic sense. That to me is mere voyeurism. The voyeuristic tendency in our culture has no place in the worship space. I can't take too much of a pastor's gushing about her or his personal life, her husband, his wife, kids, stories, jokes. What I'm talking about is real honesty about questions, the mystery of God, the doubt, the confidence, the love and passion and sense of adventure. It's not so much about bringing personal examples to the sermon or emotionalism or therapy-gone-public as it is about being as real about God and gospel and kingdom as I can be. And that means I can't help but show up in the room in all of my humanness. Being fully present to God and human life in the moment, naked as I can be, listening to the Word and to its reverberations in the soul—that's electric. That's singing the high notes.

Maybe for me that's why I most often preach without notes. As Bono says, doing so "tricks me out of myself"—it tricks me out of my tendency to be a performer, to write the well-crafted phrase, to move persuasively through an airtight design, to imitate the greatness of a preaching hero. Naked and without notes, I am unable not to be true. Before God. Before my people. Before myself. That's freedom.

14

Hospitals (and Those in Them) Need the Word of God

When I began my work as a pastor, I didn't mind visiting folks in the hospital. It wasn't hard to be nice, friendly, and upbeat—people are generally happy when a well-mannered young pastor shows up. But I did mind carrying my Bible with me. First of all, I didn't want to be viewed as "one of those"—a Bible thumper who, in my mind, didn't know how to do anything but carry a big (and it's always big), black leather (always black and leather), gold-trimmed (always) . . . Bible. So I didn't carry my Bible, but I did carry a smile. I was nice. I held hands. I prayed. But there was a second reason I didn't carry my Bible. I remember feeling that the Bible was not welcomed in these places of celebrated technological power. Intimidating pastors wasn't official policy, and I can think of few human beings who explicitly communicated that to me. But it wasn't the people who whispered that to me, it was the stuff—the machines and facilities themselves.

It used to be that in any community the biggest, the most overstated, and the most intimidating building in town was the church. But today, the biggest, the most overstated, and the most intimidating buildings are often the medical centers. And frankly, they're far better attended than the churches. They also deliver a much more tangible and apparently useful service—they keep people from dying. Not always, of course, but for the most part they do a pretty good job. And the buildings and machines that occupy them seem to swell with pride as their place in our society expands.

When I began my ministry in and among these things of such power, the Bible seemed to be pretty out of place and, while often tolerated by the staff (who knew that a little religion often did some good keeping patients patient), the stuff of the hospital whispered that my Book wasn't nearly as important as the bleeps and blips and pokes that administered the grace of the new god of technology. I'm not being completely fair, of course; material things are not in and of themselves bad or evil—we are plenty glad for what they provide—but they are what the Bible calls "principalities and powers" and as such can slide into the place reserved for God alone. As a pastor still wet behind the ears, I truly felt intimidated by the bravado of hospital technology and shrank before it. I didn't know then that the hospital *itself,* as much as the patients I went to visit, also needed to hear the Word of God in order to be what God intended it to be—an agent of divine grace, occupying its place as servant and never as master. I think those Bible-toting pastors I early tried to distance myself from knew what I could not then see.

It's taken time to change my mind. Today, I might not always carry a Bible (though I often do), but I always carry a text in mind that I speak among all the bleeps and blips and pokes. Hosting the text there among the gods of steel and electricity and drugs and know-how is vital work. The technology no longer intimidates me, and now, even when there are doctors or nurses or administrators who don't see me and the Word I bear as a member of the healing team, I've learned to stand my ground. I've also learned that there are plenty of medical people who know first-hand the limits of these gods and who themselves long to hear the Bible read in this place that often intimidates them too—they've seen the soft underbelly of the beast that demands their homage.

I imagine that this is exactly why a little text like 2 Kings 2:12 is in our Bibles.

Those who love the Word have long known intimidation when faced with technological, military, and political power. And Israel's pastors—those who long cherished these texts of ours—were keen to keep their pastors alert to the power of the words they dared utter in public places. Between the historical markers highlighting the reign of King Ahaziah (2 Kings 1:18) and that of King Jehoshaphat (2 Kings 3:1) lies the story of a transition in the "powers" who believe they manage the world. Tucked in between the stories of these two big kings is the story of two little preachers, Elijah and Elisha. The story may well have more in mind than what I see in it, but what arrests me most is the little phrase placed on the lips of Elisha at the passing of Elijah: "Father, father! The chariots of Israel and its horsemen!" (2 Kings 2:12).

When all is said and done, asserts this little text, the real power in this world does not reside with kings or presidents or regimes or political parties, and it does not reside in the biggest, most overstated, and most intimidating buildings in town, whether they are government buildings, military installations, or medical centers—no matter what their bravado would have us believe. Rather, the power to manage the world is uttered by those who faithfully tend the Word of God. Elijah, the courageous and often lonely prophet of God, who knows stunning success and terrifying fear, desperate depression and a recovery worth singing about, is the nation's true "father" and is a "technology" greater than any possible political, military, or . . . medical power—as benevolent and helpful as it might purport to be.

Tedd Lyons is the veteran pastor and dear friend who once helped me see that this text wants us to know that those who host the Word are "the chariots of Israel and its horsemen!" More powerful are they than any technology—military . . . or medical. That is why the "powers" rarely welcome the Bible and those who carry it inside the corridors of power. They know that in the preacher, they face a power that will unseat them.

So today, I enter hospital doors and walk those hallways and sit beside beds and in waiting rooms and open these texts of ours. I don't stand and shout the Word—it's a power that doesn't need my strength or my energy. As I do, I not only see the persons who need this Word leaning in, but I sense the walls themselves bending near. Not always—sometimes they still deride those who gather around this flimsy little book. But *we* are "the chariots of Israel and its horsemen!" The real weapons that bring wholeness and peace are not machines but *words*, as small and feeble as they may seem. And all we have to do is to mutter them.

73

15

Preaching and War

In the spring of 2003 as American troops began their push toward Baghdad in the opening days of the Iraq war, a cartoon in the op-ed section of the paper showed a father, glued to war coverage on TV, being chided by his little boy: "TV is making you desensitized to violence; now give me the controls and go outside and play."

The images of war captivate us. War enthralls and there are few who can resist its seduction. Though it is frightening, grotesque, cruel, and even evil, it nevertheless thrills, excites, intoxicates, and captivates—not only warriors, who can find the act of killing a rush of near godlike power, but also those who look on in admiration or disgust. War is like pornography; it's hard to take your eyes off its nakedness even if you think it's a perversion of what is good and right. It's little surprise that the ancient

Greeks, aware of the lure of war, put Aphrodite, the goddess of love, in bed with Ares, the god of war.

This lure of war is necessary for war itself. War needs this draw in order to live, and states exploit this draw to fuel their wars. If they can keep us gazing on its shameless nakedness and occasionally grant us the godlike power to preserve or destroy life, we will remain captive to war and useful to the state.

All this makes preaching in time of war both immensely difficult and vitally important. It's hard to keep the Word and its people free from entrapment to powers that aim to enlist God and everything else in service to their agendas. It's hard but it is necessary. Preaching in time of war can have great power to help people keep their bearings amid such things, but unfortunately it can also do very little—it can even become an instrument of war itself. It's an astonishing thing in my mind that in 1944 a Nazi soldier could attend worship on Sunday, then bludgeon a prisoner to death come Monday, or that in 2003 someone in the Pentagon could name a bomb the Mother of All Bombs and threaten to drop it on Iraqi women and children . . . and there was nary a peep from American pulpits.

The early Christian preachers knew the seductions Christians would face. "See to it that no one takes you captive," wrote Paul to the Colossians (2:8). This is the language of war. He imagines us as those who could be taken as prisoners of war, captive to the way of thinking that would render us unfaithful to Jesus Christ and worthless as his witnesses.

As at any time of war, preachers had a tough job to do in the spring of 2003 during the first days and weeks of the invasion of Iraq. Our job was to keep the story of

Jesus firmly in the minds of our congregations when their minds were lured moment after moment with images and sounds of war. We read texts like Colossians 2:8–15 as we watched U.S. troops moving north from Kuwait toward Baghdad. We were, amidst all the media noise, trying to listen to Paul, a pastor to a group of Christians who were themselves trying to live by the story of Jesus in an intimidating and alluring world. We were trying to listen in on the Colossian congregation as they tried to keep their imaginations captive to one thing only: Jesus Christ and him crucified. And as the troops neared Baghdad and the unpredictable battle that awaited them there, we preachers read to our congregations the story of Jesus's push toward Jerusalem. The collision of these Sunday texts with the images holding our attention for the rest of the week made for a striking juxtaposition.

We preachers were leading our people in Lent, and as Lent neared its final days our job was to keep people's minds focused on this Jesus who, while the troops rode toward Baghdad, had begun his own long-awaited campaign to take the capital city and liberate its people from tyranny. We preached Jesus's battle plan to move from east of the city, from a position on the Mount of Olives. From there, we preached Jesus's tactic, sending some of his men to gather what he needed for that final march into the city. Then we preached that march, our minds full of images of soldiers atop tanks, while Jesus rode the final and triumphant mile as Jerusalem's conqueror and the people's liberator on the back of a donkey. We preached Jesus who came into the city and dared to take it as one completely unarmed, except for the power of his voice. And we preached that by week's end, Jesus was dead on the cross, his voice and project apparently silenced, and the tyrant still in power and the people still captive. We preached the power of violence and war to strike down good intentions.

But we preachers knew that wasn't the way things would end. And with our preaching we worked to unseat war's grip on us as we testified to Jesus who "disarmed the rulers and authorities and made a public example of them, triumphing over them in it" (Colossians 2:15). We preached Jesus who, unarmed and with only his voice and body, disarmed them. We preached the cross that defeated them, his resurrection that vanquished them and proved them impotent against the power of Jesus Christ.

None of this made much sense in the larger world around us, where tanks and bombs and guns and planes and the words of politicians and generals loomed large. But we preachers knew that what makes sense "according to human tradition" may well not accord with Christ. "See to it that no one takes you captive," said the early preacher—not even the most rational and realistic arguments (Colossians 2:8). Preachers, by our words, tease the church loose from all that would take us captive, we aim to form a people who live "according to Christ." But that kind of work is never easy, especially in a time of war. In a time of war, Christians can't help but have war on and *in* our minds. And that means that we will live with a collision of images that work on and in our minds. Which ones will hold us captive? Which ones will claim our obedience? And how are we to live responsibly in this violent world that seems to require violence in order to create peace? How are we to live in a world where tyrants rule and terrorists attack and armies amass, where guns kill children in our cities and disease can be used as a weapon against the innocent?

77

Preachers will be lured by the same images that lure everyone else. We will be glued to our TVs. We will be tempted to yield to the force of war itself, embracing violence in order to defeat violence. We will want to take up arms ourselves. But holding fast to this story that has captivated us, we will be unable to shake ourselves free of the gospel that declares that the world is saved—that we are made safe and receive the peace of a just world—through the ministry of the One who disarmed the violent without violence, who died before he would kill, who loved and refused to give in to hate. And we will arm ourselves only with this word of truth, so apparently fragile up against war and all its machinery. But we, who are conformed to the One in whose name we preach, realize that preaching, rightly done, does violence to violence itself. It mercilessly unmasks its arrogance and mercifully challenges our fatalism.

Our preaching is war on war itself. Preaching must be dared; it is the one great cause.

Wednesday
A Prayer before the Word

On 2 Kings 5:1–14
February 12, 2006

There are always other remedies—
    If one doctor can't fix us we'll find another.
    If one diet won't trim us down . . .
    If one medication fails us . . .
    If one support group fails us . . .
    If one religion fails us . . .
        there's always another.

But there are times when we run out of time,
    and resources,
    and options,
    and our desperation presses us to choose an
      option
that's a real gamble but it's the only shot we've got.
    No time for another doctor . . .
    No time for a different diet . . .
    No time for new pills . . .
    No time to research a new support group . . .
    No time to find a new god to pray to.

When that time comes, give us, we pray,
    some "young girl from Israel" who can point the
      way,
    some little one who knows more about what
      counts

than those who think they know,
some insignificant one who says,
"If only you could get yourself to the God of the
    Bible,
you would be healed."

Maybe you've already answered our prayer;
Maybe she's already among us—
    speaking through this little book today,
    pointing us to the God of the Bible—
        a puny, plain, and unsophisticated witness
against the splendor of the other powers of this
    world.

But maybe, driven by our desperation,
directed by some little witness who knows where true
    healing is found,
we'll give up on "the rivers of Damascus"—
those lesser remedies—
and go down into the Jordan . . .
Humbled and obedient at last,
we will be made whole . . .
according to "the word of the Lord."
May it be so.

Amen.

16

Wednesdays—Reading the Agenda(s) of the Text

Wednesdays require the recognition that there are no innocent texts in the Bible. Every word, sentence, and page has an agenda. And so, Wednesday's exegetical work is spent trying to discern the mischief this text wants to do among us come Sunday.

When it comes to exegesis, it's right to ask about the role that biblical criticism, the modern science that's ruled the field for a couple hundred years, plays in our work. Here's my answer: honor the contributions of historical criticism, but keep its influence to a minimum. It is useful, but must not overshadow your exegesis or intimidate your interpretation. So many of the historical-critical tools are leftovers from a modern world that wanted a high level of certainty and credibility when putting the Bible up against the encroachments and challenges of scientific discovery. When overused, these tools make exegesis a slave of another master—exegesis will be ruled by the need to defend the faith or adjust the faith or make it relevant to the children of Schleiermacher's nineteenth-century "cultured despisers of religion." I'm not suggesting that some of that kind of work is not worthwhile, but I am saying that I don't find the Bible to be much interested in that. I don't think it looks in that direction at all.

Wednesday follows Tuesday's chasing of words with a couple of hours spent discerning as best I can how Sunday's text wants to form the people of God. "Lord, why this text? Why, among so much other material, was this little piece included in the Bible? I know it's not innocent, but I'm not yet clear about what it's guilty of trying to make out of your people." These are the kinds of questions I'm asking on Wednesdays. They are, to use a premodern word, "catechetical" questions—and I think they are the ones that ought to drive our exegesis, especially on Wednesdays. Sadly, catechesis has been caricatured by our culture that celebrates autonomous individualism and maligns catechesis as the meaningless repetition of another's outdated words or beliefs. Catechesis *is* about repetition, but it is *not* meaningless or outdated. It is about a community learning to echo the sound of its source—the Word of God. (Catechesis comes from the Greek word *katecheo*—*kata* meaning "according to" or "like," and *echeo* meaning "sound." My friend Ed Searcy and I stumbled on this one day in the Wired Monk Coffee House near his home in Crescent Beach, British Columbia. We may have been wired, but I've a hunch our discovery wired us back into the durable life of those monks who once formed Christians for astonishing and robust witness in the world.) Just as musicians and athletes learn to pattern and reproduce essential sounds and moves from an expert, so catechesis reminds us that disciples learn to follow Christ by echoing what they see and hear in the Bible and from the life of a congregation whose life together is increasingly being formed by the Bible's vision of life.

On Wednesdays whatever historical criticism I practice I put to use for the larger task of what I call "catechetical criticism." To my knowledge no one's ever used that language for exegesis, though I'm sure many have done exactly that in their work. Catechetical criticism means I am paying close attention to the intentions, interests, agendas, and the ideological bent of the particular text. And catechetical criticism understands that all of this is done with the purpose of forming a people who can carry out the mission of God—echoing the *missio dei* in their lives. Catechetical criticism requires of the preacher a working knowledge of the contributions of historical criticism, but it demands far more. Catechesis is deeply and demandingly pastoral, just as these texts are deeply and demandingly pastoral. They were first offered by pastors—and they have been cherished by pastors—all responsible to utter the word among a community in such a way that the community can learn to echo its own response, improvising on that word in as many different ways as there are disciples who hear it.

Continuing my example from Monday and Tuesday, "exegesis for preachers on the run," I come back to the text from 1 Samuel 4. My Wednesday work at catechetical criticism meant that after a few hours I had a sense of what I thought this text wanted to do among a people who were willing to read it and risk being changed by it. I had a sense of the way the exilic context of 1 and 2 Samuel hinted at its agenda. In the land of Empire, these ancient pastors were working to form a people who could fly under the radar of those in power and whisper a word of hope in a situation dominated by the threat of death, a people who could easily have succumbed to despair. And so, to a people dominated by the great temples and palaces that defined the world in Babylonian imperial terms (imperial politics, commerce, religion, and military might), these pastors told this little tale about an unnamed mother and a handful of midwives. Imagining Israel as so many women whispering among themselves and for the future of their people was a daring maneuver indeed!

My Wednesday meditation led me to wonder about the way this text called Israel to echo the odd ways of God in the world—to live in contrast to all that was going on around them. I imagined these pastors preaching out of their daring hopefulness that their congregations might learn to echo the witness of these women with their own lives. And I hoped that if I could just host this text in a similar way among my people come Sunday—people who deeply want to live the way of Jesus but who find that way hard to live inside a new empire—if we could just hear this text again, then I too could hope that this ancient word might have a new chance with us and that our part of the world just might echo the God who wills to be heard through the lives of those living inside any imperial hegemony working overtime to usurp the place and power of God.

17

How Do I Organize This Stuff for the Sermon?

Somewhere after the main burden of exegesis is done and before the discipline of writing begins, a "form" either begins to emerge or we preachers find ourselves casting about for a form or design that helps us organize the message that's rising up before us. The sermon begs a shape for delivery.

Of course, in the day-by-day practice of preparing to preach, the question of form, structure, or design rarely puts itself off until the second half of the week. Usually it's intruding right from the start. From the moment you've read Sunday's text, your mind begins working to order the stuff you're thinking, seeing, and feeling about the text. But ordering and forming the message must not take over—it's part and parcel of the process, but it mustn't drive it. Too often it does.

Preachers, anxious about preaching on Sunday, can move to forming the sermon for delivery too quickly—do that, and the sermon's in jeopardy; the message of the text and the way it wants to be preached by you and among your people will probably get hijacked and taken places the text may not want to go. There is a real sense that these texts have a life of their own, a mischief they want to perform and that may differ from what you want done. They are not easily controlled. They want, as I said in an earlier chapter, to "crawl out all by themselves." Your job as a preacher is to allow for that—even more, to give the message permission, to stand back and watch it emerge. You are midwife, not mother; the form of what's coming into the world is not entirely yours to shape, though you do play a very important role—important enough that if not for you, the message might never see the light of day.

Most of us have not been taught to take up this kind of posture before the text. Most of us, nurtured within modernity, were taught to believe that we exercise high levels of control over the world around us. Consequently, we preachers were duped into believing that we possess more control over biblical texts than we do. That unhelpful sense of control comes at our work from two fronts—the influences of both modern science and its handmaiden, theological liberalism.

First, Newtonian cosmology, the centerpiece of modern science, persuaded us that the universe is essentially a great clock or machine that we not only can figure out but also can control, manipulate, and fix. But from Neils Bohr, Werner Heisenberg, and Albert Einstein on, the new scientific break with modernity's cosmology urges us to stand (or better, kneel) before the mystery of the universe with a great deal more humility and wonder than we're

86

used to. Chastened by the new discoveries of quantum science, our old, modern efforts to control the vastness of creation seem not only silly, but also dangerous. The universe is wild, free, untamable, yet all the while invites us to participation and the kind of relationship that is creative—even while resisting our efforts to engineer with any real certainty our desired outcomes. We are players in creation, but never masters. We have a role, but that role is looking very different from the role modern science once envisioned for us.

Such talk of a cosmos characterized more by relationship and partnership than by clockwork precision moves us toward this stage of sermon preparation—organizing the material. We've spent the first half of the week in exegesis and by now probably have a clearer sense of the text, the mischief it played long ago when it was offered by Israel's rabbis or the church's pastors in order to shape the missional life of God's people. We've also got some inkling of how the text wants to work among our people today. But how will we now present it? What form will it take?

There are ways of answering these questions that will keep us living inside the modern world and handling these texts of ours crudely, even abusively. Wanting greater control over these living texts, and wanting it now, we won't let them "crawl out all by themselves." Rather, like a teenager in a tide pool trying to force a rock crab out into the open with a stick, we'll slap some stock sermon form on the text, thinking that by it we'll get the message out. Do so, and we may be left with only a shell—the living creature gone or dead. Modern science, while giving us many gifts—even for biblical exegesis—must be held critically and used very cautiously.

87

There's a second influence on our work that is every bit as troubling as the uncritical use of the tools of modern science—the intrusiveness of theological liberalism. Modernity, that intellectual cul-de-sac that wanted us to believe ourselves to be godlike, possessing a control over the universe meant only for the Creator, also gave rise to the theological liberalism that governs so many of the habits preachers on both the left and the right of the theological spectrum practice when it comes to forming the sermon for delivery.

During the eighteenth, nineteenth, and twentieth centuries, the claims we voice on Sunday mornings became increasingly hard to justify in the light of modern scientific discovery. Threatened by the challenges of science and following the father of theological liberalism, Frederick Schleiermacher, we preachers did what any modern person would do, we took charge. We took charge and learned to control the presentation of the Christian faith, crafting persuasive speeches that proved the relevance of these often embarrassingly ancient texts, and made the gospel intelligible or, as we'd say today, *marketable* to the children of Schleiermacher's nineteenth-century "cultured despisers of religion." This was certainly true among the liberal and mainline churches of the past. Today, it appears that conservative, seeker-driven congregations have emerged as the new proponents of an approach they have no idea is indebted to a liberalism they have no intention of perpetuating.

Liberalism, even in its conservative manifestations (maybe especially), handles the biblical text as a gold mine. Dig out the precious ore, and toss out the dross. Then take that nugget of gold and hammer it into shape for sale in a store far removed from its native setting and to buyers who don't care where it came from; they care only for its presentation. "Liberal" preachers work to mine a principle from Sunday's text (something like love or justice or peace, how to develop your spiritual life, or what you ought to do to build a strong family life this week)—something that sells in today's market. "Liberal" preachers take that principle, quarried from an embarrassingly ancient text, and hammer it into a proven rhetorical form that helps them preach relevant, palatable, well-packaged sermons for sophisticated religious consumers. They take a theme and weave it through a handful of points deftly illustrated along the way. They fashion a speech, persuasive and relevant, designed to prove that God makes sense and that Christianity can be practiced by just about anyone.

If the purpose of the church is to build big, successful, relevant churches that are attractive to the masses, then this method of organizing the material works and works well. And it appears to have worked well inside modernity's form of Christendom. But in the so-called postmodern, post-Christian world, where truth claims are up for grabs, sweeping metanarratives are ridiculed, and the church is increasingly decentered and disestablished, the translation of these ancient truths into thought forms intelligible to contemporary North Americans seems to me to be misguided. What we need is the immersion of our people into the counterworld of the Bible. Our aim in preaching is not publishing universal truths through well-crafted persuasive speeches, but forming the witness, the church of Jesus Christ as the chief argument for the truthfulness of the Bible. And for that, we must keep our congregations close, very close indeed, to the peculiar form of these texts we host week in and week out through our preaching.

Given these intrusive challenges, how do we organize our material for delivery? We let the text show us. The

Bible is marvelously rich in genre and metaphor and rhetorical strategy. But we cannot see its richness if we've lived our lives looking at the text as merely a mine of golden nuggets for us to harvest.

"Let the text itself give you the form for your sermon," I tell my preaching students. It's far more willing to do so than most of us have been led to believe. "But how?" they press me. "How do we see this new way if all we've been exposed to is the mine-the-gold-and-hammer-it-into-shape approach?"

"Seeing" is precisely what it takes, and seeing can't be bullied by a hurry-up-and-figure-out-how-to-present-the-text sense of the week. Take my work with 1 Samuel 4, for example. It took three days of dipping into the text—dwelling in its rhetoric, teasing out the meaning of its words, discerning the agenda of those who'd tendered it among their congregations long ago. It took till Wednesday midday for me to begin to see that the ancient rabbis who cherished this story were not only describing a world of seismic and threatening change, but were acknowledging the fear, bewilderment, and intimidation their congregations felt in such a setting. The story, working on me, began to show me the ways the rabbis had worked pastorally to speak their people past their fears and toward living as a people of daring hopefulness. Seeing this in the text, I was then free to move toward Thursday with a sense of companionship with those ancient pastors. Monday, Tuesday, and Wednesday had made it possible for me to imagine myself taking my own people into the tumultuous world we live in, naming with uncompromising clarity the forces of death working to bully us into fear and stony silence, and then focusing our attentiveness not on the big, geopolitical movements that easily overwhelm and intimidate, but on something wondrous, small yet revolutionary—the birth of a son and the astonishing whisper by an unnamed midwife. Now I had an outline—an outline that could stay close not only to the text, but also to the very lives of my people as well. I couldn't have bought or downloaded that outline anywhere. It had to come to me. Having immersed myself in the text during the week, refusing to give in to the anxious preparation countdown, I was free to let the story rise up before me and hand me its own form for delivery.

Of course, a sermon's form differs depending on a text's genre—a psalm or a proverb will render a form different from a Gospel or an epistle. And so, I cannot tell anyone "how" to form their sermons as neatly as do those who champion the method that worked in modernity (and still works where modernity's still being propped up by those who love the promise of control). I can only hold them to the biblical text, so rich in genre, fascinating in its rhetorical freedom, wild in its many forms. Among my students, I invite them into the sermons of preachers who themselves revel in the freedom of the text. I ask them to dwell among the sermons of the early church fathers and those of medieval preachers. I detach them a week at a time from the ways they've seen the text (mis)handled. I want them to *see* differently. And over time, the shift happens. At some point, always unpredictable, they begin to see and to find themselves astonished by the way the text itself *wills* to come into the world—and they are thrilled by their own creativity in forming their sermons and by their newfound freedom in delivering them.

But some never see and prefer instead to keep hacking away, mining for cheap little nuggets while everything around them is gold.

18

When Disaster Strikes—Dare We Preach Such Flimsy Words?

Will you speak falsely for God, and speak deceitfully for him?—Job 13:7

On August 29, 2005, Hurricane Katrina slammed into the Gulf Coast, shattering levees and plunging the city of New Orleans into hell, leaving the rest of us gaping in disbelief. Nature's irony, intended or unintended, could not be missed. Just before the storm, the debate over science curriculum in our public schools had reached a fever pitch. A groundswell of Americans now wants creationism taught alongside evolution. It's not far from the battle fought a century ago, though with new terms like *intelligent design* it seems to take on a new air of intellectual sophistication. President Bush, while careful not to fully commit himself, urged that Americans ought at least to be able to decide for themselves. Into the heat of this summer battle, Hurricane Katrina broke. Two days into the disaster, National Public Radio's Daniel Schorr framed the situation in stark terms:

> As President Bush cut short his vacation by two days to deal with the catastrophic effects of Hurricane Katrina, he might well have reflected that if this was a result of intelligent design, then the Designer has something to answer for. Rarely in my [eighty-nine years] can I remember—aside from world wars, the Holocaust, the plague epidemic—so much grievous pain visited on the human species by human beings or by forces beyond their control. Drought, flood, and famine, a deadly tsunami, war and insurrection. . . . Are hurricanes part of some intelligent design? (*All Things Considered*, August 31, 2005)

If you would only keep silent—that would be your wisdom!—
Job 13:5

Events these past years, so brutal in scope, seem to refute faith in God—Christian or any other. Events so reckless and terrifying belie any intelligence or Designer at the hub of the universe. How do we dare preach God in the face of such bewildering pain? Schorr's challenge is serious. The elderly have lived through other tumultuous periods, but even an octogenarian would be hard-pressed to name a more demanding time. And no one retirement age and younger has ever seen anything like what we've seen these last few years.

I've not trudged through the floodwaters in New Orleans or walked the ashen streets of New York City. I've not carried the dead from trains in Madrid or London, or grieved among the desperate victims of the Asian tsunami. But none of us are insulated . . . not anymore. I know people who've been in such places, and I myself have stared into the eyes of families devastated by their own catastrophic loss—loved ones hurled to their deaths as a plane plummeted to the ground. I've held their hands and searched for words to speak into their darkness.

So these three men ceased to answer Job.—Job 32:1

Words fail times like these. Let us be clear about that. There are times when it is best to be silent.

But Job said, "Am I to wait, because they do not speak?"—Job 32:16

Yet there is a place for words. There is need for words. Elihu, that ancient mourner who sat down alongside Job, speaks for us all, testifying to that longing for words that rises up inside the human heart. Words, the right words, are as needed as any aid, any rescue. And to my thinking, in spite of the challenge disaster might pose, it is the words of the Bible that speak best in times like these—for they were written in the midst of such times and were cherished by those who've lived through them. The Bible is not about escapism. It doesn't speak words that are a mere ticket out of earth and into heaven. The Bible is about earth. It is about the pain of those who dwell here. It is about the brutality of persons and nature. It has little to say about whether or not a hurricane is part of some intelligent design. But it has much to say about the God who is ruggedly involved in the world, even suffering with and for the world.

The Bible is about this God who wills peace for the world. It is about the God who saves the world, not by tossing a life preserver from above and pulling those who find it to safety, but by coming alongside, entering the storm, and carrying all creation toward the newness that is sneaking into the world. In the face of disaster the earth waits speechless. Is there anyone who will speak for this God? Is there anyone who dares to speak the apparently flimsy words of the Bible into the storm?

I must speak, so that I may find relief; I must open my lips and answer.—Job 32:20

We may not be brave enough to speak with much authority when disaster strikes. I think that's a good thing. Loud, strong pronouncements are in my mind tinny; they are, for all their bravado, shallow. Now is not the time for certitudes—it is not the time to justify God, to explain God's ways. God doesn't need an apologist, and frankly, all attempts to justify God against such devastation and despair will only be seen as absurd.

So what are we to do? I know this; we must speak—though not immediately. Silence not only honors the magnitude of catastrophe, but gives us room to return to our Bibles. But we cannot remain silent for long. We will find relief in uttering the name of Jesus Christ. We answer the storm with words that seem so flimsy against the merciless onslaught of forces whose rage is inexplicable. We offer no absurd explanations or trite attempts to clear God of charges of injustice. Instead, we dare to lay alongside the stories of devastation and despair and rage another story that knows the same pain and injustice—and that gives no easy answers. We keep our preaching close to Jesus Christ. For his story no longer seems so far removed from our lives. Jesus Christ and his suffering are no longer so opaque. He is seen with new eyes, and he becomes a companion in pain and a token of hope. We read Christmas, we read Lent, we read Good Friday and Holy Saturday with eyes strangely seeing what we never saw before. And we are pressed toward Easter, now truly daring to hope that it really isn't just about lilies and new clothes and warm thoughts of bunnies and chocolate.

Disaster can make the church more fully biblical. Preaching when disaster strikes can help us all know what it means to wait for the God who is born among us in the darkness of our night. Preaching can enter that place where we've stared death in the face, believing God is dead, and wondered how anyone could ever have called this Friday "Good." Preaching can go here and then tilt us toward a new sense of wonder. Activated with new words floating among the flotsam of devastation, our imaginations can begin to linger over this news of life breaking loose out of death, and we wonder if it might actually be true that something new and good is coming. *Because* of preaching we can live our, at times, intolerably long Saturday, positioned somewhere between the cross and resurrection, and grow in our trust that on these flimsy preached words, now become flesh among us, God dares to build a new world. And these flimsy words just might tutor the church toward the place it's meant to live— not inside its safer sanctuaries or in trying to foist some half-Christian ideology into public textbooks, but in the middle of the city, where pain is most severe and hope is most absent.

19

Preaching Jesus Up Against the Jesus of Suburbia

What often passes for Christianity may be religious, but is not Christian—not yet at least (and one wonders if it ever will be, given such a start). Culture-Christians are not terribly interested in the Jesus of the Bible who said such silly things as, "Love your enemies, do good to those who hate you, bless those who curse you, pray for those who abuse you. . . . Be merciful, just as your Father is merciful" (Luke 6:27–28, 36), and, "If any want to become my followers, let them deny themselves and take up their cross and follow me" (Mark 8:34). No, their god is not the One who says such outlandish things; their god promises safety, security, and abundance—in short, the American Dream. Jesus of suburbia.

Culture-Christians and the churches that form them will never see things this way; their Jesus has been fashionably refashioned to be the god of safety. "Jesus died to get me to heaven." "Jesus wants me to get others to heaven."

"Jesus blesses the guns and bombs and planes and policies that keep me safe and happy until I get there." So much of this non-Christian Christianity is really about creating a safe world where I'll never have to love my enemy, deny myself my creature comforts, or die as a witness to Jesus Christ. This is *a* gospel, but it is not *the* gospel.

On August 23, 2005, the BBC reported that the Rev. Pat Robertson said on the *700 Club* television program: "You know, I don't know about this doctrine of assassination, but if he [Hugo Chavez, President of Venezuela] thinks we're trying to assassinate him, I think that we really ought to go ahead and do it. It's a whole lot cheaper than starting a war, and I don't think any oil shipments will stop." Venezuela is the fifth-largest oil exporter and a major supplier of oil to the United States.

Up against this and so much more we stand to preach the Word of God. And this "Jesus of suburbia" may be among the most resistant of the world religions to our preaching. Nevertheless, week after week, year after year, we break open the Bible among our people, disentangling a worldly Christianity from the tales, fables, and myths of a broader culture that too often brokers the ubiquitous texts that seek to claim our allegiance. And while we preach, we preachers are disentangled too—for none of us can hope to live safe from the entanglements of so many alluring counterfeits that masquerade as the real thing.

I don't want to be misunderstood. I am not about bashing culture. But I am concerned that the church has preachers who "rightly explain the word of truth" (2 Timothy 2:15)—that is, the church has someone who knows which Text it is that claims us out of all those texts that would too easily tame us. Nor am I interested in making the preacher more important than others in the congregation. But I am interested in championing the fact that there must be a text handler present in the congregation (it may well be that the best, most faithful text handler is not the pastor, but some old, wizened woman who can keep even the preacher straight by her clear-eyed allegiance to the Word).

The church cannot be otherworldly—escapist. Nor can it be simply and uncritically worldly. When it becomes so much like the world, when it fashions God, gospel, and kingdom in terms of the gods and gospels and kingdoms of this world, when no one can look at the church and see Christ (in all his otherness, even as he is amid the world) but instead only a mirror image of its broken, suffering, and corrupt self, then the worldly church has failed.

But if the church is *worldly*, secular in the sense that it is truly immersed in the pain and struggle and suffering and corruption of the world, without turning over its identity to the formative forces of so many other words, and remains a community whose way of life and outlooks can only be explained by the gospel it preaches, a people whose way of life is truly cruciform, then it will be truly like its Lord, the Word become flesh. In this way, the church is to be worldly and secular in the best sense of the word, and in this way, the Word of God is preached to the world—not down from on high by some angry charlatan who wants to call down fire from heaven, but from among the people, as one of them, in love, humility, and hope. The rightly worldly church, the evangelically secular church, will always be subjected to the weakness, corruption, and suffering of the world. Only so can it be the disciple of Jesus Christ. This kind of church (the only kind of church God knows) needs preachers who keep it wholly in the Word and rightly in the world.

20

Change and Conflict— To What (or Whom) Will You Lend Your Voice?

Change is one of the few constants in pastoral ministry, and conflict, the partner who can't help but tag along with change, is an unwelcome certainty. I don't know any pastor who *likes* conflict—though some are better at facing it than others. No matter how hard or far we run, we pastors are never more than a few steps from change and the conflict that comes with it.

There are periods of calm in a congregation's life, as in a society's. But we're not in one of those periods today. Most pastors I know are exhausted. Leadership is taking a high toll on our marriages, our relationships with children and friends, our bodies, our souls. There's not a one of us who can deny that the church is living through a period of unprecedented turbulence—a state of perpetual whitewater in which the predictability and security of Christendom's stable past is a thing of the past. The trouble is, we pastors weren't trained for the post-Christendom, postmodern, post-9/11 renegotiation of the church's vocation that is our task today. And in the midst of the turbulence, we find ourselves pressured by equally anxious and bewildered church folk, many who would like the church and world to be as it once was.

Christendom is collapsing. So is that form of political empire that was built on values and assumptions that if not confessionally Christian, were at least amenable to the people in our churches. In that more stable world, we pastors learned skills and competencies that once worked but are not so useful now. And now, the assumptions and practices shared by most of us who once lived life at the end of modern, Western liberal democracy—a world in which technology and technique promised us leverage to solve nearly every problem—are sucking air. It's little wonder that we feel as if we've had the wind knocked out of us.

In this new setting, dealing with change and its lackey, conflict, are paramount pastoral skills. They are both best met through our preaching.

My own congregation, like every other, has experienced its own barrage of change-provoked conflict. I've learned, through considerable and costly failures, that the presenting symptoms of conflict are never the source of the pain our people are experiencing. Battles over the color of choir robes (no kidding), music styles (big surprise), vandalism to our property and how to deal with the threat of a community in transition around us—and most recently, increasing pressure in mainline churches to ordain

101

practicing gays and lesbians—have touched a raw nerve in the lives of our people, a people who as much as their pastors are weary, exhausted, and confused by the dizzying changes sweeping through Western culture.

But if there's one thing I've learned about pastoral ministry in the midst of such a season of collapse, transition, and emergence, it's that pastors, while fearing change, must not retreat from it. The conflict brought on by change is a gift to the church—for through conflict our fears are exposed, our reductions of the gospel are set before us in bold relief, our captivities to old compromises are cracked open (even if only by a hairline fracture), and the Word of God summons us to enter an uncertain future with new and daring obedience. Conflict is a summons to newfound freedom in the gospel precisely because all *that* is brought into our midst because of change.

Recently, during a congregational gathering called to brief our people on issues before our denomination, a person said, "If more talk about human sexuality merely leads to more erosion of moral values . . . well, then, I'll have no option but to leave the church." His wasn't a lone voice. I knew others were adding their assent inwardly. Here was an exposed and raw nerve. And here was a challenge directed initially at me: "Don't go there, pastor," the voice was saying, "not if you know what's good for you."

If I didn't believe that there are gifts for the church in this kind of conflict, if I thought that it is my job to manage this threat into submission and smooth over the conflict, if I was unaware of my own anxieties awakened by the threat, I could easily have lent my voice to either medicate the wound by aligning myself with his particular party, or worse, I could have returned the attack and aligned myself with yet another.

As a pastor, neither is my job. Rather, my job is to know my people, to listen, listen, listen for hints of the symptom's real *dis*-ease, and then recover my vocation as a preacher, lending my voice to God, and meeting that *dis*-ease with the gospel.

In this case, beneath the presenting symptoms of anger and ultimatum—past these conditions shared by so many— is the pain of a family in turmoil, a marriage in crisis, a teenager on drugs, a boss that demands too much, a nation's borders that are dangerously permeable, an economy that's chipping away at our buying power, a war gone sour, a government flailing about for some kind of political traction. In short, beneath the anger and the threat is a deep, inner awareness of a world that is collapsing. The speaker was not so much threatening me as he was begging me: "Do you have any Word from God for me . . . us?"

I could lend my voice to a particular moral absolute, and that would quell the fear for awhile, shore up the erosion until the next shell hits and more of the modern world crumbles. But I don't see my job that way. My job, and yours, is to enter this season of change and engage conflict—conflict pregnant with new missional possibilities—and preach the Word.

For help in this, my frequent companion is the prophet Jeremiah. I dip often into this biblical book that swings rhetorically around two major literary sections—each matching the pastoral and missional needs of my people. Chapters 1–25 give voice to the experience of death and grief among a people whose world is collapsing. Chapters 26–52 speak that same people into new freedom and a new world they cannot see but must engage by faith. Here are words first lent to those living in the wreckage of the exile; words that name the mistaken management strategies of Judah's religious and political leadership; words that summon the people of God to trust the Word of God to birth new forms of community life; words that beckon a band of pastor-preachers who intentionally and regularly enter an alternative reading of our current situation—one others in their anxiety simply can't see.

Jeremiah says to me: you are a preacher of the Word (1:9), mind your business. The Word will "pluck up and . . . pull down . . . destroy and . . . overthrow" much that is currently cherished. But it will also "build and . . . plant" (1:10). That's a promise.

And so, at that congregational gathering and to my anxious flock, buffeted by change, conflicted, and ready to fight for firmer footing, I said: "I wonder what all these texts we've read together all these years—hundreds, even thousands of them—might say to us. I've a hunch that they'd like us to remember that Jesus Christ is more interested in leading us into the truth than we are in finding it. I'll bet you half-believe that. There's a part inside each of us that believes that the truth of the Word of God is big enough to take care of itself. So, in the days ahead, whatever they hold for us, let's let that half inside each of us that trusts Jesus Christ with his own Word preach to the other fearful half within each of us. The Word will win. It always has." By doing so, I drew them into their faith, into the texts we share rather than into their own fears—texts written in faith during other times of turbulence and chaos; texts cherished in faith by those who'd been carried by them into the future; texts that can do the same with us who live by faith today.

Living here as a preacher, endeared neither to one party nor another, is a knife edge, to be sure. But such is the Word of God (Hebrews 4:12). Why would I ever lend my voice to anything less?

Thursday

A Prayer before the Word

On Genesis 1:1–5
Baptism of Jesus, January 8, 2006

Three great threats pressed in upon those who first
    listened to this text:
    darkness, wind, and water.
At night, their lives were particularly vulnerable;
against the storm's fury, they were powerless;
the ocean's wave, terrified them beyond measure.
This last year we were made once again like the
    people of this text—
    these threats pressed in upon us and made us
      afraid and bewildered;
    they chastened our pride and arrogance,
    our silly confidence that our knowledge
      and technology had at last given us control over
    the elements.
Water, wind, and darkness proved mighty against our
    puny presumption.
They taught us that we are not the masters,
    and we felt a new threat of chaos larger than most
    of us can remember.

As the world turns to a New Year, hoping 2005 was
    only a short but painful season,
we, your church, turn to this text and trust its
    promise that—
    that no matter how terrifying are hurricanes and
    tsunamis,

no matter how destructive are earthquakes and
tornadoes,
no matter how worrisome is the threat of global
warming,
no matter how unsettling the instability of the
global economy,
no matter how ugly the divisiveness of national
politics—
we, your church, testify to your act of creating the
world—
you moving over the chaos of the darkness and
the swirling waters,
you breathing your holy wind,
you overcoming all threats of chaos and destruction and disorder,
you bringing instead goodness and order and
beauty.

Against every threat we might face you bring a new
and holy three—
the water of rebirth,
the wind of life,
your word of command.
And whenever these three are present the world is
renewed.

Renew us today and every Sunday—
when we, with all your church, move toward you
through the water of baptism,
when we, with all your church, call upon the wind
of your life-giving breath,
when we, with all your church, listen for the Word
of your command.
Renew us in the grace that is Sunday,
the first day of creation,
the day you took charge,
the day we stop in Sabbath trust of water, wind,
and Word,
these three that alone renew the earth.

Amen.

21

Thursdays Are for Writing

Preaching is an oral art and requires us to choose words more fitting for the ear than for the eye. That said, for me it is the act of writing—seeing words on a page—that turns me round the corner toward Sunday and preaching the text I've studied the first half of the week. Thursdays are for writing. And Thursdays are often the highlight of my week of preparation.

Fred Buechner—that masterful writer—once said, "After forty years of writing books, I find I need to put things into words before I can believe they are entirely real." That's why I write. And I wonder too if that's not the reason we've even got a Bible. Moses and the band of prophets, the sages and those whose prayers we call Psalms, Jesus and the apostles too—all preached in one way or another. And yet, either they or someone else put their words down on the page. Writing is an indispensable part of preaching—not just to give words durability, but also to make them real. After twenty years of preaching sermons, I find that writing things down helps me believe things I might not otherwise come to believe. That's no small thing for a preacher.

I've always written as part of my preaching discipline, but too many of my preaching years I spent wringing my hands over the words I tried to put down on the page. During those years, I didn't like Thursdays much at all. Dissatisfied with so much of what I wrote (it was rarely good enough in my mind to match the prose of those I felt compelled to imitate), Thursday felt like it never ended. Thursday had a habit of trespassing on Friday, and unhappy with what I wrote on Friday, I carried the chore into Saturday too. It was a rare dawn on Sunday that didn't find me still fussing with it all.

Somewhere about the tenth long year, worn out, frustrated, and my family in tatters because I was never able to be present and free on Saturdays, I determined to have a funeral. Either I put to death my own deadly habit of writing or, it seemed to me, I didn't have many more years worth living as a pastor. I also figured that if I wasn't enjoying writing my sermons, folks weren't likely to be enjoying my preaching of them. So I buried my old ways. I stopped struggling with words and determined to write for the sheer love of them.

I'd read somewhere in Annie Dillard's *The Writing Life* that writing is a lot like art. You can't paint landscapes if you hate the smell of paint. Love that smell, and you're well on your way to painting something of beauty. Love gives birth to art, I'd heard her say, and you've got to love words if you want to write. I loved words; I knew that. I loved what they could do. I loved what they helped me see and feel and touch. And if I loved words, I figured I could love putting them together. On top of this, take away the pressure of writing a sermon fit for making myself famous, and I figured I might be able to love writing about the text.

For a decade, that's exactly what I've done. On Thursdays I steal away from my office to a little Roman Catholic coffeehouse and bookstore—my little monastery for the day. There, surrounded by things helpfully strange to a Protestant preacher—figurines of the saints, rosary beads, crucifixes, and books about Mary and by Aquinas, Merton, and the more famous popes—I tap away on my laptop. Sometimes I just dawdle. Other times I write in torrents of words that astound me when the storm subsides. Sometimes I write a commentary on the text with little to no interest in how it will preach. At other times I write a full sermon. I take what comes and give myself gobs of freedom. It doesn't matter to me now what I end up with by early afternoon. What matters is that I was there, present to the text and to the Trinity, present to myself and to the daily experience of the people I love and among whom I will open this text come Sunday.

Let me add that my Thursdays are guided a great deal by a helpful piece of advice—something nearly gospel—from the writer William Blake. "Improvement makes straight roads," Blake wrote, "but the crooked roads without improvement are roads of genius." Now when I write, I'm no longer aiming for straight, well-engineered roads. Instead, I play. And a lot of what I write feels pretty crooked. While I can't claim that it's genius, I can claim that it's much better than it used to be. Now I love my Thursdays. That's got to count for something when Sunday comes.

22

Illustration

Illustrations have become mere trinkets, commodities bought and sold in the marketplace of religious goods and services. Slick promotional cards clutter my mailbox, promising me ways I "can touch, relate, and motivate today's media culture." Digital ads clog my email with religious spam assuring me as a preacher the power to "quickly set up your message in a way that pulls your congregation in." All I need is a subscription to sermonspice .com or any of a plethora of other illustration services, and with just a few clicks I've got access to stories and video clips that fit a myriad of situations, A to Z. Just what you and I as preachers need most. So we're told.

We preachers want to illustrate our sermons, but I'd rather we didn't—not with what passes for sermon illustration today. Not unless we can move the practice of illustration away from the hackneyed art it's become. Not unless we can talk about sermon illustration in terms that don't mimic the tactics used to sell everything from cars to beer to feminine hygiene products and treatment for erectile dysfunction. By the way we engage this business of sermon illustration you'd think we don't believe that the Bible's very interesting. By the way we illustrate, we preachers seem to be saying that this old, embarrassingly distant, hard-to-understand text requires us preachers to mine its gold, discover a useful theme, and then hammer it into a trusty form for delivery. "Three points and a poem." Or to update the phrase, "three points and a video clip."

This business of sermon illustration, though so common, actually obscures the text of scripture we hoped to bring to the light of day. Sermons preached this way may draw the masses, but I can't be persuaded that this is preaching. Speech-making, maybe. Entertainment, yes. But not preaching.

I used to illustrate my sermons this way too. There were too many Sundays for too many years when folks shook my hand or wrote me notes after worship and said things like, "You're a great storyteller," or, "That story today really moved me." For too long I liked those responses—loved them even. I got to the point where I preached *for* those responses and stewed in my frustration for a while after a sermon if I didn't get them. Sometimes I'd ply my wife long enough Sunday afternoon till I got one. It got rather pathetic.

But over time the frequent compliments grew thin, and something began to gnaw at my preacher's conscience. I began to realize that people loved the stories I told, the illustrations that populated my well-crafted sermons, but showed little evidence that they were growing in their love

111

for *the* Story. They were increasingly dependent on my words, but not on the Word. That troubled me. I began to long for someone to come out of worship, shake my hand, and say, "Preacher, that *text* came alive for me today, and I don't think I'll be able to shake it off. It's disturbed something inside me, and it may well take the week to make some kind of sense about what it wants to do to us as a church." I began to figure that if I could get that kind of response, then we as a church might really be on our way to being the people of God.

Thankfully, I do get that kind of response today. So do the other preachers who host the Bible among our congregation. In fact, there's much less talk about our congregation's preachers today than there is about this Bible of ours. I'll say more about this in a later chapter called "Teaching Other Preachers," when I explore the way we're learning to teach the congregation itself to preach. The change wasn't without struggle; it's not easy to shift the way a congregation expects to hear the sermon. But when the change finally comes, there's no turning back. Our people, by and large, would complain about the drivel offered up for a sermon if any of our preachers ever returned to the kind of illustration that makes *stories* more interesting than the *Bible* and requires the preacher to be some kind of shaman who turns the biblical story into "chicken soup for the soul."

Here's a short summary of what we've learned together about the practice of sermon illustration—

First, *we place a premium on the stories of the Bible* and its peculiar language. Steve Varvis is one of our elders and a professor of history. I've learned a lot about preaching from him and the historians he reads. At one point Steve got me reading Robert Louis Wilken and about an epoch in history not much removed from the turmoil of our days. According to Wilken, when Augustine, the non-Christian teacher of rhetoric at the University of Milan (384 CE), came under the spell of Bishop Ambrose and his sermons, he sought baptism into Jesus Christ. "What shall I read," he asked Ambrose, "to make me fit to receive so great a grace?" "The prophet Isaiah," said Ambrose. So Augustine picked up the prophet. "But I did not understand even the first verse of the book," he wrote, "it made no sense to me." So he set the book aside "to be resumed when [he] had more practice in the Lord's style of language." Augustine—pagan, intellectual, teacher of rhetoric—understood that becoming a Christian is like learning a new language. There are no shortcuts. And so, as a congregation we follow the wisdom of an earlier age (not unlike our own): the language we ask our preachers to use is language that stays as close as possible to the language of the text. It doesn't dabble in the babble of the culture around us. It immerses us in "the Lord's style of language" and forms a people whose *lives* then become the real and relevant witness to Jesus Christ in the world.

Second, when we do tell stories from everyday life, *our preference is for stories that illustrate discipleship in our common life together*—the church living the way of life envisioned by the text. "Who among us is living the risky life of this text today?" asked Tedd Lyons, one of our pastors, in a recent sermon. "When our students at University Chapel visit the fraternities and sororities, then pray every Sunday for the students at Fresno State, they are living this text. When our elders and deacons knock on doors in the apartments around us on Saturday mornings and ask residents how we can pray for them, they are living this text."

By preferring stories of lived discipleship, we think we're following the model of Jesus, who on one occasion stopped his sermon in the temple and pointed to a poor widow putting two small coins into the treasury. "This poor widow," he said, "has put in more than all those who are contributing to the treasury . . . but she out of her poverty has put in everything she had, all she had to live on" (Mark 12:41–44). Mark, an ancient congregation's preacher, shows Jesus, another preacher, illustrating his sermon for the sole purpose of making the church a living illustration of the ways of God.

And for us, that is what illustration is all about. Ultimately, sermon illustration isn't about "setting up your message in a way that pulls your congregation in" and delivering an inspiring speech. It's about fashioning a *congregation* that is itself an illustration of the sermon.

This doesn't mean that we avoid the world. Consider this from a sermon of mine on Deuteronomy 18:15–22, entitled, "What's the Use of Preaching?"

> The advent of the printing press made books available to the masses; it loosened the control of information; it decentralized power; it made democracy possible. And these are great gifts—for as long as information is held by a few, the powerful can make docile the people, and tyranny and abuse are possible. The democratization of knowledge is essential for freedom and we ought to be concerned whenever the flow of information is constricted, redirected to a few, or even blocked. The public library, the free press, access to the Internet, and the availability of today's massive search engines, while not without problems, guarantee democracy—they are the tools of freedom. They provide us with the opportunity to make decisions, to plan, to interact, to enter the future.
>
> With so much information available to us, what is the use of preaching? And who are preachers—what is their role in society? What can we possibly hear from preaching that we

can't hear elsewhere—and hear better? Is it possible that the larger society around us is right in looking down their noses at us who gather every week to hear our preachers? Or is there something going on in the churches that cannot be read or heard or purchased or downloaded anywhere else?

In this sermon, the world is here in all its fullness. But the sermon tells no stories about the world. Nothing from *USA Today* or *Time.* No clip from sermonspice.com to hook the listener. Just a long, meandering immersion in Deuteronomy's way of forming Israel for its life in Canaan, an old, odd text that reads our contemporary experience with uncanny accuracy. The sermon continues:

> Deuteronomy is anxious over the assumptions and practices it takes to form a people who can live faithfully for God while living in a land that's hostile to or at best disinterested in their beliefs and practices. Deuteronomy's great anxiety is over the future of Israel's youth—and it is cherished by any community that knows that its children are always at risk when its adults fail to take responsibility for their own formation as followers of the God revealed in Jesus Christ.

Then the sermon ends by pondering how we as a people might practice the text—what might happen among and through us if we as a congregation were to take our preaching seriously.

> It wouldn't surprise us at all if a people like us became what Moses hoped we would become—a people "fearless" and whose loyalty to the Lord makes us a "blessing to all the families of the earth" (Genesis 12:3).
>
> It wouldn't surprise us one bit if we became what Jesus prayed we would become—those who "obey everything that I command you" "and make disciples of all nations."
>
> It'd be no surprise at all that a congregation like us not only formed the next generation of those "loyal" to the Lord,

and that from our youth might "rise" a whole new generation of preachers who can speak the Word with courage and
hopefulness.
It could be us. It will be us. So help us God.

We could be wrong, but we think the *church* is the kind
of illustration the God of the Bible is interested in. That
takes a peculiar way of practicing the art of sermon illustration. And you'll never be able to buy *that* online.

23

Street Preaching— Ministering the Word . . . Bodily

The Word of God is most comfortable on the street, and over most of the best of its history those who've preached the Word have understood this. Moses preached in Pharaoh's court and on mountains; he uttered the Word in the desert, at the edge of the sea, from riverbanks. David sang the Word on craggy hillsides, Jeremiah ranted in the streets of urban Jerusalem, Ezekiel ministered in the resettlement camps of Babylon, and Ezra in the midst of Judah's ruins. I don't need to remind anybody of the places where Jesus preached and where his disciples found the Word welling up inside them and spilling out into the world. For them preaching required a bodily witness out in the world, midst the rough and tumble of everyday life; the Word, while it did find itself domesticated from time to time inside religious buildings, was most at home out beyond them. And this kind of street preaching (the kind of preaching most of these preachers knew best) was always offered in service to forming a people who, with their bodies, made known the Word in the midst of daily life. Says Ezekiel, "the nations shall know that I am the LORD, says the Lord GOD, when through you I display my holiness before their eyes" (36:23). Street preachers from Moses to Paul all preached in order to make ready the real street preacher: first Israel, and then the church—through whom "the wisdom of God in its rich variety might now be made known to the rulers and authorities in the heavenly places" (Ephesians 3:10).

In our day, street preaching has become a caricature. Images of doomsday prophets on street corners, tract-toting evangelists working feverishly and not too differently from ticket scalpers at the entrance to a stadium, and sweaty, shrill, wild-eyed harbingers of God-knows-what fill our minds when we think of street preaching. And if most of us preachers ever think on such things, we quickly dismiss this kind of preaching as an aberration, something beneath our skills, or at the very least something a long way from our interests.

The caricature humiliates the Word, because the street is its natural habitat and street preaching cannot be relegated to the fringe of the church's life or to the most bizarre of its witnesses. The Word lives amid all the ordinariness of daily life. The fact that so much preaching and Bible study are done inside the safe confines of church buildings is a testimony to the aberration preaching has become and the degree to which the Word is humiliated in our day. Street preaching must be reclaimed from this caricature, but that doesn't mean that preaching on the street will ever be fashionable in North America or anywhere else.

The first move in reclaiming street preaching is to shift the focus away from the image of the lone preacher. The Word's ministry in the world will often require individual preachers to go out and preach in the street, for the church will need from time to time daring preachers who put their bodies into the street and on the line for the Word of God. Thankfully, we have a history of these witnesses who've popped up whenever the church has grown corrupt and the Word humiliated by its captivity inside and among the religious. But street preaching must always be done, even by a lone preacher, in service to leading the church *as a people* into the street to minister the Word. We preachers then become, not lone rangers, but members of "street preaching congregations" who take our lead and we take theirs, going together out into the homes and businesses and schools and neighborhoods, the world of hope and despair, of saints and sinners where the Word belongs and longs to be. And this, the "congregation as street preacher," is the second move in reclaiming the mission of preaching on the street today.

The Word needs a body—this we know from the Incarnation. And the Word needs to be preached bodily—we know this too. But too much of our preaching is essentially disembodied. We preach from inside the building and expect the church to go out from this building. And yet the church is already out there, in the world, day in and day out, and the Word is among them. But the way we preach hides this from the church. And when the life of the Word in the world is hidden from a congregation, we sin against the Word. Preachers, it's high time we put an end to this sin. It's high time we joined the Word and its church out in the world.

There are ways we can preach that don't push the church out from the sanctuary into the world as much as we invite our congregations to see with new eyes the way the Word is active among them every day. When we learn to host the Word of God out among them, we help them (and us) see that the world in which they live is where the Word lives. Going out into the street, preaching, we teach that ultimately it is not us, not the single individual who preaches, but that we all together, the church, the body of Christ, live in the street as the true street preacher through whom God displays God's holiness before the world (Ezekiel 36:23; Ephesians 3:10).

But let us not be naive. Street preaching is not safe. Preaching in the street, we and our people will learn the cruciform way of Jesus in the world. We will follow Jesus, "the faithful witness" (Revelation 1:5), or, more literally translated, "faithful *martyr*," in the world, for the love of the world and for the saving of the world—and that will mean from time to time being pitched into the teeth of rejection and hatred, violence and death itself for the sake of the Word's mission in the world. "The blood of the martyrs is the seed of the church," preached Tertullian to the street-preaching churches of the Roman Empire. And it's the presence of a people gutsy enough to bleed in the street that seeds the world's new day, birthed through the ministry of God's Word.

24

The Word on the Street— Seizing the Moment

I tried preaching once as a young man standing on the steps of East High School in Denver during the city's annual People's Fair—a celebration of everything under the sun. There my courage and my words were drowned out by the joyful song of the Gay Men's Chorus and the angry verbiage coming from a nearby booth that sold a multitude of bumper stickers with abrasive slogans like "Keep the Church Out of My Crotch." Years later, I went preaching with others in front of Grady Hospital in Atlanta. We claimed that spot of ground as a holy place for those living on Atlanta's streets until security came and demanded our silence. I've read the Bible with students at the Riverpark outdoor mall in Fresno and ministered the Word in the yard of a homeless shelter.

The first episode, I consider a failure. There was no church, no community, no other preacher with me; and I was not a witness speaking for a community. I was there by myself, and the powers were too great for me. I could hear them laughing above the din of everything else.

The other episodes were not bad episodes, but they were not great episodes of street preaching. I say that only now as we as a congregation are moving into what I consider the kind of street preaching the Word requires of us. My people (and I call them "my people" not because I am pastor over them, but because they are the people to whom I belong) have for quite awhile been putting their bodies on the street for Jesus Christ. They've been feeding the homeless, tutoring immigrants, and forming welcoming ministries for Southeast Asian refugees for years. Their bodily ministry on behalf of Jesus Christ has recently led them to advocate for safe and affordable housing for the underprivileged in Fresno, and that's put them squarely up against the powers of slumlords as well as out among those officials and agencies struggling to get traction against such a massive problem.

At one point, they joined with other "street-preaching" congregations in Fresno and arranged a way not only to get congregations out onto the streets of Fresno, but by doing so, also to involve those who could best address this housing blight in our city—the mayor, the city council, and the proper agencies. Congregations have enormous power when they don't stay inside their buildings.

On a spring day, we loaded charter buses with hundreds of people, including the mayor, council members, and agency representatives (as well as the media) and toured some of the most blighted housing districts of our city. After the tour, we gathered for a meeting with

122

the mayor, followed by a common lunch. Before an audience of hundreds, with cameras rolling, it was my job to interpret the moment and challenge the mayor on behalf of the coordinating congregations and the residents we were representing.

Here was the best street-preaching opportunity that had ever come to me. We were out in the world, bodily present to its great struggles and pressing needs, with other Christians from other congregations, and on property not owned by a congregation. It could have easily been no more than a political gathering. But that's not what the Christians who organized the meeting wanted it to be. They were putting their lives on the line for the gospel, out in the street; it was a daring act of faith, their own witness to the Word of God. And here I was, just one among them, but with the gifts and calling to speak on their behalf. And I could not disappoint them.

"Mayor Autry," I began,

As you know, many children in Fresno face devastating barriers because of unsafe and unsanitary housing conditions. We saw some examples of this today. Two issues in particular allow these substandard conditions to persist: slumlords and a severe lack of safe, affordable housing. We are calling on you today to continue your deep commitment to change the face of Fresno. We are not pointing fingers. Rather, we have begun by learning, firsthand, about the conditions that children are facing throughout our city. We have also been teaching tenants about their rights as renters. And now we are asking for your help and partnership in making safe, affordable housing a reality for every child in our city. Anything less is unacceptable. Anything less, is for us, a betrayal of Jesus's calling to us: "when I was hungry you gave me food," Jesus said; "I was thirsty and you gave me something to drink, I was a stranger and you welcomed me, I was naked and you gave me clothing, I was in prison and

123

you visited me" (Matthew 25:35–36). Forty thousand people are on the "waiting list" for safe and affordable housing in Fresno, and we cannot stand by and ignore the needs of Fresno's children and their families.

We are made bold today by the desperate need in our city, and by the call of God who has come among us in Jesus Christ—God, who long years before Jesus, dreamed a dream through the prophet Isaiah. Isaiah saw a city where people do not live in fear, where children do not die, where old people live in dignity, where people dwell in good houses, where those who plant gardens eat their fruit (Isaiah 65:20–25). It is a dream, but it is not too good to be true, for God wills it and will work through us until God's dream reigns in the city we love. We ask you, in God's name, will you allow us to work with you on a comprehensive, grassroots affordable housing strategy?

The Word belonged there that day. And I was its voice. But others had done the hard work; the churches had put their bodies on the line. Together we were preaching the gospel in the street, and that preaching is tilting the city toward its healing.

25

There Is No Innocent Preaching

All preaching has an agenda. There's no innocent preacher, and no innocent sermon. All preaching is local, the Word of God uttered from a place on the ground that possesses all its own peculiarities—and while that place shares much with the world around it, there is no other place like it.

Preachers are those who are biased toward their locale, women and men who are as much a part of the place of their ministry as those who hear them. We breathe the air of this place, know its dialects, enjoy its food, love the sound of its birds and traffic, can navigate its roads, and can venture safely through the unspoken rules at a dinner party. If we cannot be charged as guilty by association with those among whom we host the Bible Sunday after Sunday, our words are far less likely to bear the Word of God. That doesn't mean that I can't preach in Sao Paulo,

Brazil, if I'm from Fresno, California. Nor does it mean that a preacher from Indonesia can't preach in Colorado. You can preach as a person disembedded from the culture of those who hear you, but doing so will carry considerable risks. You can also run a marathon and smoke a pack of cigarettes a day; it's just going to be a lot harder.

Preaching is deeply pastoral, offered from among your people—biased, affected, influenced by everything that influences them. As a preacher you can't be naive about your biases. If you are, you'll come to believe that the gospel-according-to-you (which is what it always must be in one way or another) ought to be the norm for others in other places and at other times. And so, from time to time, you and your congregation will need a witness from outside, just to keep the gospel safe from your own domestication of it. And both you and your congregation will need for you as a preacher to live with some aware-ness of the forces that open you to hear the gospel the way you do, what moves you to preach it as you do, and why you are compelled to do so.

My friend Steve Taylor is to me one such witness from outside; he helps me stay clear about the way I preach, and the way I teach and write about preaching, and he helps me stay clear about why. Without people like Steve, I might be guilty of thinking I'm innocent and that what I do and say ought to be what others do and say. That might sound strange—for isn't this book a very witness to the fact that I think my ideas and practices ought to be imitated? It is, but because of people like Steve, I can also confess my desire to offer this testimony in order that others might fashion their own local theology and practice of preaching. For then we'll really have some-thing—preachers who are improvising on our vocation, scattered across the earth into those peculiar places where God has sent *them*—and no one else—as a witness.

Steve Taylor is the lead pastor among a group of people who call themselves the Opawa Baptist Church in Christchurch, New Zealand. An able theologian of international caliber, Steve is deeply embedded in the gospel at work among his own people. He knows the culture of his people, loves it and its life among them, sees both that culture's gifts for enriching the way it experiences the gospel and the way its deficiencies can be met by the gospel. When Steve hears me talk about preaching, he shakes his head and says, "You and I must preach in very different settings."

We do. I preach among an affluent, largely suburban people. A congregation begun in the late 1960s, it once worshipped at the northernmost edge of the city, adjacent to the new campus of California State University, Fresno. Today, the city has shifted, and our campus sits amid a community in transition. The growing edge of the city is now miles to the north, and we are surrounded by immigrants from Southeast Asia, Eastern Europe, the Middle East, and Latin America. Poverty, crime, gangs, and slumlords are not as far away as they once were; they are now at our door.

Fresno itself is a community of extraordinary cultural diversity. Over a hundred different languages are spoken in the Fresno school district. The rich farmland of California's Great Central Valley has inspired immigrants for over a century to make Fresno home. We face significant environmental concerns—water and air pollution, urban sprawl, and community planning that can't keep up with development.

Religiously, mosques, temples (Sikh, Hindu, and Buddhist), and synagogues dot the map but are dwarfed by the vast array of Christian churches. The Central Valley is the West Coast's Bible Belt, and California's center for a blend of conservative Christianity and Republican politics. We are also deeply influenced by megachurches, whose version of Christianity holds enormous political and cultural power. On a recent Easter Sunday, one such megachurch rented the Save Mart Center, our shiny new entertainment and sports venue. Following the sermon, a country and western singer, draped in an American flag, sang "I'm Proud to Be An American."

Welcome to my world. I know it. I love it. I struggle with it. I preach the Word of God within it.

But I can't just know my world. If I am to understand what I do and why, I must also know myself. I am a German-American. And that heritage probably makes more sense of my understanding of preaching and its practice in this place than any other single factor. It was my people whose Christianity was, by and large, incapable of resisting Hitler. In fact, it was in large measure complicit in his crimes. The German church failed to preach the Word of God when its time came to deliver. So identified was it with German culture that culture became its God, and it exchanged the Word of God for half-truths and all-out lies, words that often drew upon its Christian heritage but with a sinister twist. And few of them saw it happening.

I live not only with shame over my people's failure—the church's failure—but also with anxiety that it's far too easy to do it all again. If American preachers, and perhaps especially those of us in places like Fresno, don't keep our wits about us, we could allow September 11, 2001, to stir the kind of nationalism that was set in motion on February 27, 1933, when a terrorist attacked Berlin's Reichstag, burning the seat of German political power. There are indications that our American ignorance of history makes us terribly vulnerable to repeating it.

I also have Swiss blood in my veins. This means that not only do I have certain affinities with the German preacher Dietrich Bonhoeffer, but also for the Swiss preacher Karl Barth. While Bonhoeffer formed a community of preachers who could not only discern the dangers tempting the church and who could resist them by their allegiance to the God of the Bible, Karl Barth offered his own resistance—a blast against the kind of theology that gave itself as an acolyte to Nazi power. In his great "Nein!" to natural theology, he gave no room to the German Christian love for God's revelation in culture. It was too easy to listen to Bach, drive a Mercedes, see blond hair and blue eyes, and believe that being German was the epitome of being human . . . the best God had to offer the world.

I confess that in a culture like mine, beloved as it is, I worry about such things for my people and for myself. And in the wake of the attacks in September 2001, it would be too easy to believe ourselves to be a righteous people, and to allow conservative (or liberal) politics to persuade us that we have a holy mission, that we're on God's side. And it would be too easy for us Christians who enjoy such security and privilege to go along with it all with nary a voice lifted in warning.

There's no question that my preaching, my teaching and writing about preaching is vastly different from my friend Steve's, who works in a very post-Christian New Zealand—a place where much of popular culture has no real memory of Christianity. Mine is a theology and practice born out of a sense of crisis—a desire to loose us from the easy belief that God really is more American than anything else, and even more, from the assumption that God is a Republican or a Democrat. Mine is a desire to keep God and the Bible free from such dangerous accommodations.

Mine is also a theology and practice that, because of that urgency—my own inner and often unspoken anxiety—lacks an awareness of God's goodness in creation, the beauty and gifts of culture, a sense of wonder in the second book of revelation: nature. People like Steve keep me open to that. People like Steve keep the gospel safe in my hands. They won't allow me to live only in my particular understanding of the gospel and the way I preach it.

That said, I stand by my conviction that the theology and practices offered in these pages are what the church in my setting needs. I also trust there's enough right in these pages to help outside preachers improvise on it in their own settings. Of course, it won't fit exactly the situation in your part of the world. So, consider me your own "outsider" who can help you keep the gospel safe in your place and among your people who receive your own weekly testimony to the Word of God.

We're never innocent, but together maybe we'll keep ourselves honest, and maybe we'll keep our preaching free to be what it must be if this world is to be saved.

Friday

A Prayer before the Word

On Luke 24:1–12
Easter 2004

We have stood and sung of Easter,
    and our songs feel good to us—
    they speak of life and hope
    and your saving power.
But in an hour or two,
    their goodness and rightness and hopefulness
      will be sorely tested,
    and some of us may wonder if Easter is nothing
      more than whistling in the dark.

We will be reminded . . .
    of fresh threats of attack,
    of hostages and soldiers and civilians
    in harm's way,
    of cancer entrenched
    against our best efforts to defeat it,
    of skyrocketing tuition costs,
    of fatigue and depression that saps our energies.
Death, and its effect on our world,
    ridicules our glad songs of Easter.

And so,
    knowing what will come
    when you send us out again, we pray—
        speak us out of our Friday fear of death,

speak us past our Saturday anxious waiting,
and speak us into
your Sunday power to save.

Give us your Easter Word,
and let us be Eastered today—
in hope against a world dragged down by despair,
in courage against a world that denies your
miracles,
in tenacity against a world
that would talk us out of daring faith.

Easter us today in newly found freedom
to "get up and run";
to "see and return home amazed"
at what you have done in Jesus Christ.

Amen.

26

On Friday, "Preacher, Stop and Listen"

As the week draws toward its end, it's time for the preacher to shift from the active, rational work of thinking and writing to a much more intentionally receptive and prayerful posture before the Word. Having focused on the text Monday through Thursday, the preacher sits before its Author on Friday and Saturday.

For most preachers, Friday and Saturday are crunch days. Quite often the week's countdown presses preachers to hunker down as best they can and get that sermon ready. Some preachers are quite competent to get done what they need to get done working this way. But most of us aren't. And I'll go out on a limb and say that I don't think any of us should work this way as a course of habit. Some preachers might be able to cram sermon preparation into the last two days of the week and preach well occasionally, but I don't think they can do so consistently. Jesus congratulated Mary and challenged Martha and in doing so put preachers on notice that they who would lead their people into the mystery of the Word can best do so only when they've stopped fretting in the kitchen and have plopped themselves down for a while before the Mystery himself. A simple strategy for shaping a normal week of preparation enables preachers to move toward the weekend in a way that fosters just this.

I realize that it runs counter to the way many of us work our weeks, but doing so is more consistent with the nature of our work. Origen and Augustine, Aquinas and Anselm, Luther and Calvin, Bonhoeffer and Merton all understood that there is a spiritual and contemplative experience of the Word that no preacher can neglect. Unfortunately, we in our day have become so enamored with so-called communication excellence and its corollary, the terribly seductive Siren called "relevance," that many of us strain right through till the time we preach, trying to find just the right words or joke or story or video clip. We enter worship breathless and sometimes so proud of ourselves and what we've come up with that we're not much good to God and the people God wants to form according to the Word.

Great communicators are a dime a dozen. And we don't need more of them. It's not terribly difficult to please the masses, to entertain, to fill time with what amounts to little more than religious "spam." It's not hard to run off half-cocked having spent very little time really listening to God. A rereading of Jeremiah 23 does wonders to cure me of my desire to be among them: "Thus says the LORD of hosts: Do not listen to the words of the prophets who prophesy to you; they are deluding you. They speak visions of their own minds, not from the mouth of the LORD" (23:16). So warned, on Fridays my most important task is to simply plop down before the Lord and *listen*.

Of course, things intrude into the life of a pastor that a pastor can't control or neglect—there's a death in the congregation, trouble in the staff, a wedding or community obligation that loads things up and compresses sermon preparation or threatens to overrun it completely. Yet even on those occasional weeks when things have run amok and I find myself scrambling to find time to pull a sermon together come Friday, I prefer (instead of anxiously fretting and grinding away trying to get something down on paper fit enough for preaching on Sunday) to pause instead, radically abbreviating my normal exegetical routine, find some solitude and silence, and just . . . listen.

In listening, the real sermon is born. In listening, the preacher is changed from being a mere reporter of things observed to being a messenger. A sermon is not a poetry reading or a lecture or an exhibition of great oratory skills—it is a living word. And if I am to utter this word, I must be sent from the Word. I must have dwelt long enough in the presence of the Word to yield up my own will and fears and imaginations. Like dirt held in the hands of the Creator, I am raw material; everything I've done has fertile potential but is not yet what it might be when the Breath comes and gives life (Genesis 2:7).

Two prayers guide me into this exercise in listening. First, I pray playfully the conversation between our Lord and Peter, and invert the dialogue (John 21:15–17). "Lord, do you love me?" I ask. "You know I do," comes the divine reply. "Then, Lord," I dare to pray, "feed my sheep." Of course I know what John intends here. The dialogue put his way is a word *to* us preachers. But on Fridays *I* need to have a word with *the* Preacher. I take license with John's words and take this audacious step because on Fridays I want to get this preaching thing right. Speaking with God this way asserts what I better remember—I cannot feed the congregation on my own. Asserting that, calling God into the task, I am then ready to listen so that, having yielded my life in service to God, I can now take what I hear and pass it along. I am better able to obey Jesus's words to Peter, "feed my sheep," if I have faith that God is at work in my preaching as an active partner.

The second prayer follows on the first. The prophet Jeremiah is the preacher's companion because we have such a complete record of his struggle to live up to the difficult pastoral task assigned to him. And it is to Jeremiah's words that I turn most often to help me as a preacher. My second prayer on Fridays seeks to hold God to God's promise: "God, you say to me, 'If you utter what is precious and not what is worthless, you shall serve as my mouth' [Jeremiah 15:19]. Well, here I am. You have my ears. And here is my mouth, my lips, my tongue, my breath, my mind . . . you may use me as you choose." In this way I'm praying that Friday (and the coming Saturday too) will be for me and for all the church's preachers (and here I pray myself among that great mystic band scattered across the earth) a furnace of transformation, where we are purged, refined, pressed down, shaken, and stood up again on our feet, readied to serve as the very mouth of God.

I'm not a hermit on Fridays. A part of my Friday is spent tidying things up from the previous days of the week. I look over the worship plan for Sunday, return e-mails, make a few pastoral calls, check in with staff. I also try to get home by mid-afternoon and give myself and my fam-

136

ily some semblance of a weekend. But I give the first and best part of the day to listening to God, yielding myself, dropping my agendas, stilling the many competing voices that chatter at me like crows in a tree.

This Friday focus may require as many as several hours. Regardless of the amount of time I yield for this, I nearly always come out of my Fridays with a much clearer sense of what the Word wants to do among us come Sunday. And when I don't—and there are those times when things, because of my own soul's lethargy or God's own stubborn elusiveness, remain confused and unsettled inside me—I leave Fridays having wagered that, come Sunday, clarity will come. And when I've bet on God and kept faith with that gamble, I've never been disappointed.

27

Dissent from Death— Preaching the Funeral

Tomorrow we'll bury Frances. She's a congregational saint. When our people talk about what it means to make disciples, they point to Frances. It's not just for her life lived so well that we'll remember Frances, we'll remember her for the way she died. Frances died well, and dying well may be her greatest living testimony. Three months ago, when she first learned that the disease that was making her life difficult would probably kill her, the two of us talked openly about death. She steeled herself, looked at me, and said, "Jesus Christ never promised that we wouldn't suffer. Jesus never promised that we wouldn't die. He promised us power to face death, for death won't have the last word."

Tomorrow we'll bury Frances, and Sharon Stanley will preach. She'll know just what to do with the Word—or better put, Sharon will know exactly what the Word wants to do among us tomorrow. She's a skilled preacher who knows how to host this Bible of ours at a time when death will try to draw suffocatingly near to us and leave us gasping for hope. Because of Sharon and preachers like her, I can honestly say that death doesn't stand a chance. It's not that death's ignorant; it's proven itself to be awfully resourceful over the years in its refusal to give in to the power of life. Nor is it foolish. Death is belligerent. Tomorrow, not only will it face the testimony of Frances's dissent even in death, but it will face Sharon's dissent in the midst of life. In its belligerence, death's not reckoned with these two gutsy women whose testimony will gather a congregation of the living around the Word of Life, and when all is said and done, another congregation will know how to speak its own daring dissent. And even death's belligerence is no match for that.

All this is what we preachers are supposed to be doing when we show up and open up our mouths at a funeral. But this is not always what we do. Death confuses us; it wants us to lose our bearings. It would like us to forget what we are supposed to do at the funeral and instead would have us do any of a number of lesser things. Two of these lesser things come to mind.

On the one hand, confused by death, we easily fall prey to efforts to sentimentalize death. Death loves sentimentalism because there is nothing that the sentimental can do to dethrone death. Pastors know the lure of sentimentalism. We know how easily the funeral can become something more like a Garrison Keillor *Prairie Home Companion* episode than a bracing challenge to the powers of death. We know how easily things can get out of hand and the service balloon with stories, schmaltzy solos, and homemade videos designed to pull from us as many warm smiles and happy memories as they do tears.

On the other hand, we also know how easy it is to give in to the pressure to manipulate. Who among us hasn't been pressed with the appeal, "Pastor, Aunt Mary wouldn't have wanted a single person here to leave without having the chance to make a decision for Christ." And it won't be long until we're asked by the state to manipulate death to serve its purposes. Our government, struggling with a war gone sour, can't afford to let scenes of our war dead turn public opinion. We will be asked to frame death in defense of the nation as the highest honor; we will be asked to preach our dead sons and daughters as martyrs in the cause of democracy.

I don't want to be misunderstood. There is a place in the funeral for memories and favorite songs and DVDs. There's a place to call people to decision. There is a place to frame a life in terms of honor and even martyrdom— but never on behalf of the state.

Tomorrow, Sharon will step up to preach in the face of death. She will lift her voice in dissent from death—its claims, its agendas, its lies and wiles and ways. She will lead us all in the chant: "Death has been swallowed up in victory. Where, O death, is your victory? Where, O death, is your sting?" (1 Corinthians 15:54–55). Yes, we'll then be readied to face our own Frances-like deaths, saying in our own way, "Death will not have the last word."

And we who preach will open our mouths at the funeral to ensure that death doesn't have the last word.

28

Preach Christ, Not the Deceased

I've said that the funeral sermon is the voicing of our dissent from death. What, then, is the relationship between the sermon and the eulogy in the funeral service?

The eulogy is a time of reflection on the life of the one who's died, and this takes many forms. Sometimes there's no one in the family who is willing to speak in public, and so it falls to you, as pastor, to collect the stories of the person's life and weave them into a meditation that honors the life of this child of God. (Sometimes it's easier than others, depending on the character of the deceased, the knowledge you have of this person, and the willingness of the family to talk.) The eulogy might also take the form of a few witnesses coming to testify to the life of the deceased. Often (depending on the culture you're in) there may be an open time in which members of the assembled congregation may stand and speak a memory or word of gratitude.

Unfortunately, in many services there's a tragic and unhelpful confusion of the sermon with the eulogy. Too many preachers combine the two, with the unfortunate result that there really is no exposition of the Word. There is instead an exposition of a human life. Make no mistake, that single human life must be honored as a gift from God (even if that life's been spent recklessly and the dead is a scoundrel). But that eulogy, vital as it is, is still not a sermon and ought to be kept separate from your preaching.

Some preachers may be alarmed by my insistence on keeping these two messages separate. Did not God in Christ *join* the divine and the human? Might we, by separating the sermon from the eulogy, rend asunder what God has joined? It's true that God has marvelously and mysteriously joined our humanity and made it holy. And we must not dabble in Gnosticism by the way we handle the funeral. Bodies count. Humanness matters. The Word was and is made flesh.

That said, I still insist that if we confuse the sermon and the eulogy, a sentimentalizing of the deceased can too easily take over and eclipse Jesus Christ who is the humanity of God. By doing so we actually impoverish our understanding of what it means to be human. Separating the sermon and the eulogy doesn't mean that we refuse to mention the deceased during the sermon—that would suggest that we must protect God from ordinary life (a very Gnostic move itself). Instead, we preachers will keep to our peculiar business: preaching Jesus Christ, the New Human Being, and by doing so gather the dead inside that story. Our humanness in life and in death is gathered

142

inside the divine. Through the new humanity, the new creation most gloriously and mysteriously and subversively revealed in Jesus Christ, God assumed our humanness in order to free us from the dehumanizing power of death. The author of the Letter to the Hebrews preaches that Christ shared our humanity "so that through death he might destroy the one who has the power of death, that is, the devil, and free those who all their lives were held in slavery by the fear of death" (2:14–15). We are made most human by Jesus Christ, and if we preachers don't bear witness to *that* reality—if we relinquish the marvel of our peculiar work at the funeral—there are precious few others who will.

Believe me, keeping clear about these things is a real gift to the preacher when the dead person's a rat. But it's also a gift when the deceased is a saint. Our calling keeps us clear about what's most needed. People will want us to preach the person, but what they want is not what they need. The time for remembering will come. But when we stand to preach, that time must be put off for a little while yet.

Here's my advice: always put the sermon up front, after a hymn or song and before the eulogy. If you don't, you will have lost the day, and the service will tilt heavily toward humanism—sometimes a wondrous and marvelous humanism, but with little of the gospel. So, preach Christ and preach about ten minutes, as hard and clear as you know how, about the triumph of God over death. Then let the service take its necessary turn toward the person. That human life is now gloriously framed by that one Human Life (God incognito) who himself tasted death that might we hear his Easter shout and rise with him victorious over the power of death.

Death would love to help us write our sermons, turn them into eulogies, and keep them focused on the dead. But the dead, as good as they may be, cannot save us, and preaching them isn't what we preachers are about.

29

Fear of the Other—
Preaching as Disarmament

Among the chief tactics of the fallen principalities and powers is the incitement of fear. Our world is rife with fear, perhaps now more than ever. Our post-9/11 world knows fears we've not known before, especially among those of us living in the Western and Westernized world where we once believed ourselves to be invincible and secure, and where fear was minimal. Churches, of course, are not free from fear. In fact, our own fears beget our own dirty little wars that lead to forms of coercion and conflict and abuse—you don't need me to teach you about this, you know it well enough. Our dirty little wars (and our big ugly ones) begin with our fear of each other, a fear that is, at bottom, a fear of death.

Not long ago a handful of us opened up one of the church's dirty little wars and ran headlong into the tactics of the powers. I hosted a conversation around the theme "Homosexuality and the Future Church." After the customary niceties and framing words and stepping around the elephant in the room, we found ourselves moving rather quickly into frightful places. Gay and lesbian Christians were finally able to express their fear that the words and ways of straight Christians were no different from what they have experienced from so many others outside the church—an effort to silence them and dismiss them: as one participant voiced it, "to erase me." Straight Christians voiced their own fears that gays and lesbians, and those who support them, were trying to "stuff things down our throats." It astonished us that our conversation could awaken words that evoke images of terrible violence. We had touched the raw nerve of fear—our fear of the other. And it wasn't much different from the myriad of other fears that plague our world and lead to such terrifying violence—fear that another might take what I have or hurt those I love, fear that another might get more than I get, fear that someone else will do better than I will, fear that the other might be right, fear that I might be wrong, fear that I may have to change because of my encounter with the other, fear that I may have to become vulnerable, fear of being undone because of the other. Behind these fears lurks the power of death, the power to erase me or stuff something down my throat, and, in the end, kill me.

The Bible's first book teaches that this fear of the other is the chief effect of sin's entry into the world. Cain became angry and jealous of his brother Abel. His fear of being erased or outdone or overshadowed by his brother drove him toward violence and murder. The first move of the "sin . . . lurking at your door" (Genesis 4:7) was to

146

incite fear of the other. And xenophobia, as the chief tactic of the fallen powers, has plagued us ever since—racism, sexism, nationalism, and a host of other phobias, including homophobia, are all born of its sour fruit, and nearly all phobias end in some form of violence. Even when a phobia doesn't end in violence, it lives by the threat of violence.

Fear may well be *the* moral problem in the Bible, the source of all other moral problems. The Bible places fear and violence at its beginning. And at its end, the Bible shows them as undone in and through Jesus Christ. Throughout the Bible it is that holy whisper, "Do not fear," that weaves the narrative together, guiding it toward its consummation in the new creation.

Observing the world, and observing it through the text as we preachers are supposed to do, it seems quite possible to me that the devil will lure us to focus on lesser moral issues. And I wonder if my own tribe, American Evangelical Christianity, played right into this in November 2004 by focusing explicitly on the moral issues of abortion and homosexuality and ignoring the implicit moral issue driving all else—our fear of the other, and in particular, our rising fear of those who hate us and wage war against us. It was this fear above all other fears that put Bush back in the White House. My neighbor spoke for many American Evangelicals when he said, "Bush will keep us safe; the rest of the world should be grateful that we're willing to fight the terrorists."

There is no good news in this. Fear and our enmeshment in it is old news. We play fully into the devil's hands, and we fail to embody the newness of the new creation, the kingdom of God. At Christmas 2004, Archbishop Rowan Williams reflected on the nature of this world of fear:

147

No one could or would deny that we face exceptional levels of insecurity and serious problems in relation to an unpredictable and widely diffused network of agencies whose goals are slaughter and disruption. It is not a mistake to be concerned about terror; we have seen enough this last year, in Iraq and Ossetia, of the nauseating and conscienceless brutality that is around. But some of you may remember words used at the end of that worrying and wide-ranging television series in the autumn, *The Power of Nightmare*. "When a society believes in nothing, the only agenda is fear." We struggle for a secure world; so we should. But what if our only passion is to be protected and we lose sight of what we positively and concretely want for ourselves and one another, what we want for the human family? We are not going to be living in the truth if we have no passion for the liberty of God's children, no share in the generosity of God.

The tactics and stratagems of the fallen powers rely on the incitement of fear whenever possible. Surely they revel in our current world situation. But in their revelry have they forgotten that God has preachers on this earth? Or is it possible that we in our preaching have put up such little challenge to the powers that *we* are as good as forgotten? I think the powers know what we can do with our words, but I don't think we always do. So long as there is one preacher and one congregation who host the Word of God week in and week out, there is a foothold on this planet for true liberty. So long as there is at least one preacher, and at least one congregation who welcomes her daring speech, the powers will tremble in anticipation of her preaching that describes the disarming actions of Jesus Christ who "disarmed the rulers and authorities and made a public example of them, triumphing over them in [the cross]" (Colossians 2:15); Christ, who through death "might destroy the one who has the power of death, that is, the devil, and free those who all their lives were held in slavery by the fear of death" (Hebrews 2:14–15). Formed by Christ's witness, both preacher and preaching congregation become a force for disarmament on the earth—for we who trust in the generosity of God need never bear arms because we are afraid of the other or because we've behaved in such a way that the other fears us. The generosity of God begets true liberty; we preachers are its heralds, and our words are its champions.

In Jesus Christ death and fear are undone, unmasked, declawed. Preaching simply tells that truth. But that doesn't mean we will live unafraid. Few of us have seen the full fury that fear and death can throw at us. We preachers and our congregations will live betwixt and between the Word of Life and the powers of death, and we will not always be faithful to the gospel. We may well pick up arms in a church meeting and play into the devil's tactics. We will lean away from Jesus Christ, and our preaching will serve the violent agendas of the state. We may ourselves, pressed into the frightful embrace of terror, kill another. Bearing arms is never right for the Christian and is never good. Taking up arms always gives the powers another foothold on the earth, another day to reign. When we give in to violence of any kind, we always sin and will need to repent, return to the Word of God, and reclaim the only thing that will make the powers tremble, not cheer—the ministry of *preaching*.

We cannot defeat death on death's terms or by its tactics. All weapons, save one, will find their way, regardless of every good intention, into death's own arsenal. "The sword of the Spirit, which is the word of God" (Ephesians 6:17) is the only weapon we preachers can own, and it has nothing in common with conventional weaponry (2 Corinthians 10:3–4). God came preaching when there was

149

only chaos. The prophets came preaching when political and military powers had made a mess of things. Jesus came preaching armed only with the Word. The apostles too came preaching, naked except for their words.

What will we preachers do in a world so full of fear and violence? Will we come preaching, trusting the sacred power of these words become Word? Or will we trust the hard steel of the powers and cowardly arm ourselves with something more "practical"?

30

Preaching at a Time of National (or Any) Election

The presidential election in the fall of 2004 pressed American politics to a fever pitch. On the positive side, the democratic process was in full swing—more people voted than at any time in American history. Negatively, because so many believed the fight was of such massive consequence, we didn't just press the boundaries of political decorum and ethical practice, we fell headlong into mudslinging, underhanded tactics, and abuse of power. In the midst of all this, I found myself digging into our biblical texts not only to keep my personal bearings in the midst of the fray, but also to stay clear about my work as a public preacher. In times like these, it is no easy task to form congregations that remain more serious about discipleship than about the party affiliations and political opinions that could easily divide them.

Our congregation was reading the lectionary texts from 1 Timothy and 2 Thessalonians on Sundays during the heat of the fall campaign and election season. Timothy provided us with strong words about the kind of pastoral leadership that stays clear-headed and forms the people of God in the midst of empire. Thessalonians nourished a durable hope in Jesus Christ, who is coming again to reign in spite of the intentions of the usurpers. These texts, read over us and hosted each week by our preachers, helped us place our hope in Jesus Christ amid all the vain promises and endless words of campaign ads and convention hoopla. They directed our hope to Jesus Christ alone but never urged us toward noninvolvement in the political process. No, during that intense political season, they told us that the best way to be involved, the best way to serve America (or any nation) was by being the church. Disciples first. Americans and Democrats and Republicans and whatever else, a distant second.

That's not terribly easy. And we struggled with it. In the fall Republicans and Democrats weren't slow to declare that God was on their side. The conventions of both parties were replete with such swagger. And had we not handled the Bible the way we had, if we had allowed the Bible to be co-opted by partisan politics, we might have swallowed the shallow rhetoric, split into factions, each side assured of God's blessing.

To identify Christian faithfulness with the Republican or Democratic or Green parties is, well, preposterous . . . worse, it's dangerous. Not long after the presidential inauguration, the Republicans were breathing easier; they felt saved and hopeful. The Democrats were licking their wounds, shaking their heads, and wringing their hands. But for the church, Advent, Christmas, Epiphany, and Lent were coming, and the preaching texts would be up to their usual mischief among us—dragging us away from our petty loyalties and allegiances and into the life of God in Christ. Plunged deep into God's way of saving and ruling the world, we Christians would have no time for political smugness or despair.

It was the Temptation of Jesus (Matthew 4:1–11) that called us to discipleship that first Sunday of Lent—a strong text that preaches Jesus's courage in the face of alluring economic and political temptations. It is also strong in its intent to reorient the disciple-church away from trust in worldly power and toward the cruciform way of Jesus in the world. As we explored the text that first Sunday of Lent, the devil throwing temptations at Jesus and at Jesus's church, I was the day's preacher, and I said: "It's little wonder that we don't believe the way of the cross will work. There's so much in the world—so many other words—that tempt us to believe that the way of the cross may get us to heaven but won't get us far on earth." The text was up to its mischief with us, and I'd planned my own bit of preaching mischief—before the service I'd placed a TV, a laptop computer, a magazine, and a newspaper in various places throughout the sanctuary. And as I spoke, I began carrying these things from their places out among the congregation and plopped them down unceremoniously on our Communion table that stands front and center in our worship space.

One by one the objects crowded onto the table of our Lord, overwhelming the chalice. Finally, I walked out of the sanctuary to the narthex and carried the American flag back into the worship space, toward the table, and planted it right alongside. It dominated everything and towered victorious and proud before us all, urging us all to do what we've done since childhood—pledge our allegiance. I didn't need to say much more, so I said only this: "Matthew, pastor to a disciple-community, wanted his church to know that at the outset Jesus too faced forces that wanted to talk him out of the cross. At the beginning of Lent, with so much going on in the world around us, this text wants us to know that we face these forces too. Matthew taught his church to follow Jesus and speak into the face of all those vain promises three simple words: 'It is written.' He wanted them to believe that on the confession of those three simple words God's new world is born." Then I asked worshippers to enact those words. I invited several volunteers (they were not prepared in advance) to come to the table and remove these objects to their proper place in the sanctuary. "None of these objects is bad. But they aren't in the right place. They crowd out the Word and tempt us to live a life other than the life of the cross. Come, remove them to where they belong, and by your action confess to them and to everything else that would crowd out the Word, 'It is written.' The Bible tells us that on this confession the church in the world takes its stand; with these few words the church does what is most helpful to the world."

One by one, folks did just that. The first few were easy. The magazine and newspaper and TV and computer were settled in pews here and there. But the flag . . . well, it stood proudly for what felt like minutes, and I worried that I might have to finish the sermon and remove it myself. But then, slowly, a Vietnam veteran rose and stepped into the aisle. Coming forward, he gently lifted the flag from its place overshadowing the table and respectfully carried it right out the back door of the sanctuary. From there in the narthex, it could both observe the church of

154

God at worship and hear the Word of God. From there in the narthex, it could no longer rule over it. From there it could decide if it would obey the Word or not.

Preaching is always risky business, and there may be no riskier time than when the nation's needs loom large. But there may be no time more important for the church to be the church and for preachers to preach the Word. When we preach during a time of national election (or at any other time of political significance), we preach Jesus Christ and by doing so form congregations loyal first to Christ, and who therefore can hold their political affiliations loosely. It is terribly easy for preachers to unwittingly allow the Word of God to be domesticated and nationalized—and there's been too much of that tomfoolery in recent times. But it's far more than tomfoolery, it's a sin against Jesus Christ and his church; it puts the church in danger, and if the church is in danger, then so is the nation. For what the nation most needs is the church, God's new nation among the nations, herald of hope for the world.

I'm no longer surprised by what a church can do and what ordinary disciples can dare when they're freed up to encounter the Word, when because of the freedom of the Word they're not hunkered down in the cramped space of their party positions. When we preachers refuse to let these texts of ours become domesticated, nationalized, and occupied by foreign powers, we give the Word the freedom it requires, and we help give the disciple-church the freedom it needs to keep its loyalties straight.

Saturday

A Prayer before the Word

On Mark 5:21–43
Fourth Sunday after Pentecost 2006

You said, "daughter, your faith has made you well."
You said, "daughter" . . .
to one who'd been called "patient" more times than
she could remember those past twelve years.
You said, "daughter" . . .
to one who'd been poked and prodded by baffled
    medical students
till they each walked away awed
by a true textbook case of medical mystery.
You said, "daughter" . . .
to one whose mother had long since given up
    praying for her child.
"Daughter," you said,
and that could have been enough to relieve her
    suffering.

But you said more.
"Your faith," you said, "has made you well."
"Well"—finally . . . after the experts had written her
    off.
"Whole"—finally . . . after such endless, weakening
    bleeding.
"Healed"—finally . . .
    by "faith."

By "faith"—that desperate lurch past the crush
   of so many other able bodies;
by "faith"—that last-ditch effort to touch even your
   shirtsleeve;
by "faith"—that silly gamble, that crazy hope, that
   wild interrupting fantasy . . .
that maybe you,
possibly you,
certainly you and you alone could cure her.

Could it be, Lord Jesus, God among us,
could it be that our faith can make us well?
Bring daddy home?
Put food on the table?
End a war?
Stop an epidemic?
Awaken the church to be more than a broker
of religious goods and services?
Could it be, Lord?

"Have faith," you tell us.
Well, then, you'd better show us how.

Amen.

31

The Word at the Wedding— Why We Don't Preach Marriage

There are two things I try to keep in mind on those mornings, those occasional Saturdays when I awaken and turn my mind toward the wedding sermon. You may have your own short list too. I hope you do—for fixing a firm sense of purpose for our preaching is vital on these days when the busyness, the many anxieties of those involved, and the multiple cross-purposes at work on the wedding day can splinter our abilities to concentrate on the preaching task at hand. If you've got your own list, you may find we're on the same page. If mine are different from your own, well, you'll either enjoy arguing with me or take something of mine into your own. Either way, I'll be pleased enough—you'll have left this chapter clearer about your particular role at the wedding.

On those Saturday mornings when I have a wedding, I begin by reminding myself of some wedding basics—that most who come won't be interested in me; that just about everyone there will have their minds on things other than my words; that people (especially those paying for the wedding) will expect me to smile, be as charming as possible, and not screw things up. I've often felt that the one thing really required of me at the wedding, what will really please those in charge, is for me to avoid coming across as the kind of doddering dolt many people expect of that aging profession, the clergy. I remind myself on those mornings that, for almost everyone, the sermon's not the big event. Finally, I tell myself that, when all else is said and done, I'll have less than ten minutes to preach Jesus and invite people into the partnership that is his church.

This is not the most encouraging way to start the morning—this humiliation—but frankly it's just the kind of gift I love to give myself as a preacher. The expectations placed on the wedding sermon are terribly low. And that sets me on a high. For when it comes to those ten minutes (give or take a few) when I play host to the Bible's own voice at the wedding, there are few who are braced against it. If there are any walls erected against the Word of God, at the wedding they are thin, gloriously thin. Because of that I have the chance, with just a handful of words, to sneak up on nearly everyone with words that might just rouse even the dullest attender toward faith in Jesus Christ. The humiliation of the Word and its preacher is for me a treasured freedom. Reminding myself of these things, I'm now unencumbered enough to put myself to the task of getting clear about exactly what I aim to do with those ten minutes of freedom.

First, I'll want to host the chosen biblical texts in such a way that folks come to terms with the evangelical fact that the focus of marriage is not marriage itself, but Jesus Christ. Luke 14 is probably not the best text to preach at a wedding: "Whoever does not hate . . . wife and children . . . cannot be my disciple" (14:26). The mother of the bride would not be amused. Nevertheless, Luke 14 provides a hermeneutic we preachers ought to employ if we are to think of marriage in terms of Jesus—even if we're preaching Genesis 2 or Song of Solomon or 1 Corinthians 13 publicly.

If we preach marriage itself, handing the couple a few principles for living their marriage, we set the marriage on flimsy footing. The ideal of marriage cannot hold couples through the rigors of life together—as current divorce statistics can attest. Preaching marriage makes marriage an idol, and I've found that the love of marriage—or rather, the need we have for our marriages—can make us hold too tightly onto them. A tightly held marriage too often becomes oppressive, manipulative, even abusive. "Instead," I want to tell couples at their wedding, "if you want to save your marriage, you must be willing to lose it."

At the wedding, nearly everyone expects an idealization of marriage, five steps to a happy married life. That, I cannot give them. Rather, I must preach Jesus Christ and invite believers and unbelievers to risk his way of living, his wild, free, extravagant kind of loving. "Make it possible for them to love Christ," I remind myself on Saturday mornings, "and they'll have a chance at finding the goodness of God in marriage; they'll have what it takes not just to survive marriage, but to thrive."

"They cannot do any of this without the church," I also tell myself. And so, my second aim in that brief ten minutes is to interpret the gift of the church for marriage—the church as it is preoccupied with Jesus Christ and his mission. "You and your marriage will need the church," I'll want to tell them, "not in order to perpetuate a religious institution or to become a more moral citizen. You will need the church so that you can save your life from the bland existence of living common to most husbands and wives, parents and children, jobs and political parties, houses and cars and retirement annuities. A bland existence that needs such things to be secure and content will always lurch at some point toward disappointment, control, and eventually violence—violence toward others in abuse or toward ourselves in depression." The church alone can make it possible for this couple who'll stand before me in a few hours—and all those who listen to my words—to find a way of life that makes it possible for them to live loosely with their own needs and expectations and requirements, and enter into the adventure that is discipleship, that is, more attached to Jesus Christ than they are to each other or to their starry-eyed vision of marriage.

If I can help them love Jesus Christ and not their marriage; if I can invite them into the broader companionship of the church, then I know they've got a chance at learning to live Christ's way. Wild. Free. Extravagant. Costly. Giving up all things in order to find all things. Cruciform. Easter-shaped. The kind of marriage we need. The kind of marriage the Word wants to make.

Envisioning marriage this way may be uncommon—foreign to the lives of most of those who come to weddings. Framing marriage this way *is* uncommon because it's not *preached.* But we preachers are sent to change that; we are sent to ensure that such a vision for marriage has a witness.

32

Living with Chronic Disease— The Preacher's Teacher

Preachers are, of course, human, susceptible to everything everyone else is. Nevertheless, there are often many in our churches who want to believe otherwise. There are those who have a hard time imagining their pastor enjoying sex, sitting on the toilet, fantasizing over someone who's off limits. Similarly, there are those who imagine pastors are less susceptible to illness and disease. Few will admit to all this. Regardless, our churches are still awash with this kind of thinking. Among other things, folks really do hope being close to God might deliver them from their humanness. And pastors, apparently closer to God than most of the rest of us, are often an icon of their yearning.

It's not just "they" who think this way; we preachers may well want to believe this too. This is what can make it a crisis when the preacher's humanness intrudes into ministry. Disease, for example, is one "thorn in the flesh" that often feels more prickly for us preachers than it might for other, less public folk.

Doctors tell me that I'm living with a disease that I probably won't die from but will certainly die with. And they, as well as others with Crohn's disease, tell me that this disease can make life pretty miserable and, at times, make me feel like dying. I've had a few bouts with my disease that suggest they're probably right. I suppose I could look at my disease as an enemy. I did try that path, but it didn't last long. Frankly, doing so didn't help; treating my disease as an enemy put me at war with my body. What's more, it put me at odds with some pretty remarkable people I've known over the years who've taught their pastor a thing or two about bearing disease and living with dying. My body's already at war with itself—that's the heart of the immunological disorder that is Crohn's. And my body doesn't need my mind to make war on it as well. Add to that truth the witness of the body of Christ, the saints who invite me to see my disease alternatively, and I'm learning to embrace disease as a teacher, to find Christ and to find myself in the disease.

Being sick, chronically sick, being told that sickness will be a life partner, has forced me to do what I would otherwise not do—reevaluate my lifestyle, diet, daily rhythms, and the drive that's not only gotten me where I am today but has also wounded my body and could wound it further if I don't listen, learn, cooperate. Disease has forced me to admit my vulnerability publicly, to receive care from my congregation, to trust in and rely on the gifts and strengths of others, to learn to do less, not more. But I am a troublesome student. I admit that "going back to school" after all these years is frightening. I feel dull, slow, inflexible. But I have a persistent teacher, one that's not going away.

Disease can make it difficult to preach. Sometimes we may need to stop preaching (and doing much else) for a season, but suffering in our humanness does not disqualify us, and I am finding it does not make our preaching as a witness to Jesus Christ less effective. Rather the opposite is true. Instead, I am learning that our humanness *qualifies* us to preach. Humanness, especially suffering, inducts us into the life of Christ, who suffers and is "effective" *because* of suffering. That we don't understand this, or welcome it, doesn't make it untrue.

My wife, a saint in her own right, chastened me one Saturday night during a period when I was complaining that being a preacher is unfair, that it's unfair when the preacher's humanness intrudes into the preaching life.

"Who else has to stand up and preach on Sunday morning when they feel so terrible Saturday night?" I whined.

"Do you think you were qualified to preach," she said, "on all those other Sundays just because you've felt good, just because you seemed to have it all together? Because you were strong, healthy, and bright?"

No one ever preaches because they have it all together, I'm learning. They preach because the Word made flesh is borne best by our humanness, even in its humiliating weakness. It's never delivered by those who've got it all together, even when those who deliver it think they *are* strong, healthy, and bright.

Of course, we preachers are supposed to know that. But to learn that—to really become preachers—we will need a teacher who will stay with us for life. For some of us that teacher will be cancer or heart disease or Crohn's.

The "thorn in the flesh" becomes a teacher we'd best not have removed. I can't shake the impression that bearing such thorns befits those who know and preach the way of Christ. And not only does it befit us, it begets us most gloriously human, most wondrously alive . . . even while embracing these bodies of ours that are not yet abandoned by the powers of death.

33

Teaching Other Preachers

On the first Sunday of Advent, our congregation distributed its first Advent Devotional. Twenty-four of our folk hosted the text each day of the week during Advent—excluding Sundays (our congregation's shared day around the Word). They took their cues from the daily lectionary, choosing from three of the main texts—Old Testament, epistles, and Gospels. Frankly, I expected most of our people to choose the epistles (those clear instructions to churches). I didn't expect what we got—a majority of our folk chose the prophets. It's really something when a layperson is taken hold of by Amos or Haggai, treading where ordained preachers often fear to go. You might think our people naive; you wouldn't if you read their expositions. It floored me when I read them—better yet, brought me near to tears. Through their testimony I began to realize how far we've come. It's no longer our ordained pastors who know how to handle the text; there's growing evidence that we are becoming a congregation of preachers—perhaps even a *preaching* congregation who can argue for the truthfulness of the gospel through our Word-formed lives.

There were half a dozen instructions our editorial team gave our Advent writers to help guide their expositions. The fifth of these charged them to handle the text in a particular way; it serves as a handy summary of the core convictions that have taken hold of us as we've begun to teach our congregation what it means to host the biblical text, whether they write or pray or preach:

> **5. Engage the Text.** Since we want to immerse ourselves in the Bible itself, and because we as a people are recognizing that the Bible is at least as interesting and meaningful (more so, we pray) than ordinary life around us, we want you to engage the Bible text itself. Please don't write nice stories about life with a Bible text tacked on. This is not "Chicken Soup for the Soul at Advent"—you are one we trust to stay close to the biblical text, listen for the Word of God to our congregation, and tell the truth about what you hear as best as you can.

On that first Sunday of Advent, one of those writers passed me on her way out of the sanctuary after worship. As a preacher, you know the kind of things usually said during that habitual passing ritual each Sunday. Brenda cocked her head, gave me a look that disturbed me enough to worry about what might follow. Then she said, "I get it now."

I can't recall ever getting *that* from a passing worshipper. And so, taken in, I said, "Well, I'm not sure *I* do; you're going to have to tell me what you mean."

"Six months ago," she said, "I was sitting with three friends from three megachurches in town, and as I listened to them I found myself saying, 'Our church doesn't get it; our pastor doesn't get it.'" But then, with the kind of drama Brenda likes, she added, "I get it now. *We* get it now. And *you*, pastor, you get it."

These twenty-four writers are witnesses to the ways we rather informally are teaching our congregation to preach. We've also taught over a dozen people (not professional clergy) to stand on Sundays and host the Word of God. The congregation's become a little school for the Word of God—not because we preachers, ordained by the congregation for the particular task of handling this text publicly, want time off from preaching. No, we're schooling us all to host the text because that's what preaching aims to do. Preaching births a preaching congregation, a people whose way of life is formed by an intentional investment in the power of these peculiar words that can't be heard anywhere else. By sharing the ministry of the Word broadly, we as a congregation become God's peculiar rhetoric; we, as a congregation, become God's own persuasive speech.

Millennia ago, Socrates sought a form of rhetoric that would "please God best." That rhetoric is not found in a winning technique, among gifted wordsmiths or champion orators. It is found in a people, ordinary and simple, and often fearful. Sandra Eaton, an elder and one of our newer preachers, knows this: "When you invited me to share in the ministry of the Word," she tells me, "I was startled, scared, awed, challenged, but finally blessed. I'm blessed because you trust people, even the most ordinary of us. You trust *me*, and I was quite sure I didn't have the stuff to preach. You walked beside me, sharing in the journey of exploring God's Word, helping me take that great leap of faith that believes God speaks to and through all

169

who come to him." Through preachers like Sandra and John, James and Kelly, Ken and Justin, Dave and Greg, Michael and Judy, Ruth and Joe, we're not just trusting people with the Word of God, we're learning to trust the Word with people. And that's more revolutionary than any of us ever dared to imagine.

When Brenda walked out of worship that Sunday and said, "We get it now," she was referring to all this, and it filled her with awe and delight. Word's getting out that it's no longer the pastors who are "putting their skin on the table," "opening a vein and bleeding for God." There's a whole congregation that's now doing so. To my mind, that kind of congregation is the kind of rhetoric that "pleases God best"; it's the kind that's most capable of changing the world.

34

Practicing the Sermon

I remember wandering, as a young preacher, among the library stacks at a nearby seminary, looking for help with my preaching. I stumbled across an antique copy of Charles Spurgeon's *Lectures to My Students.* Vivid in my mind, even to this day, are the particular pages where he taught his Victorian preachers to practice their sermons, especially the gestures and movements they were to use in the pulpit. There were little pictures of a preacher making hand motions, complete with arrows showing the direction the hands were to move and the magnitude of those movements. These I actually practiced for a short time as I rehearsed my weekly sermons, feeling more confident about the authority those gestures and my vocal recitation of the sermon would provide for me when I later preached it before my congregation.

When I write here about practicing the sermon, I'd imagine that this is the kind of practice you think I mean. I don't. I no longer think gestures ought to be practiced, and I don't think the sermon ought to be rehearsed . . . in advance. A rehearsed sermon and gestures practiced over and over probably aren't bad things. It's just that in the first place, my sermons are never complete enough to be rehearsed, and second, the time others might spend in rehearsing them I prefer to spend getting silent, yielding myself to God, and allowing the mystery of the text to penetrate deep places inside me. I've also preached too many sermons and listened to too many sermons that have been practiced, and frankly, they *sounded* practiced—there was no real room for those departures that bring life to the preaching moment. But even more than all this, I think a sermon ought not to be practiced in advance because doing so betrays what preaching is all about. Doing so keeps us preachers and our congregations stuck in the fallacy that preaching is about the preacher's performance. It's not. Preaching, ultimately, is about the performance, the practice, of the congregation—that witness for God, formed by the preaching of the Word, who becomes the only meaningful argument for the truthfulness of the gospel this world's ever going to get.

Shifting the practice of the sermon away from the preacher and onto the congregation has made all the difference in the world among the people I serve. This last week alone, I had three independent conversations that each proved to me that it's not our preachers who are practicing the congregation's weekly sermon. Taken together, these three conversations are evidence that the weekly sermon is now being performed by the congregation itself—and that's where its practice belongs.

A little background is necessary to help you understand what's been going on. Every year our congregation focuses its life around a single practice of the Christian faith. We focus our life together in such a way that the things we practice have time to become habits, those habits we hope will in turn become virtues—a way of life that is instinctive.

Several years ago we spent the year focused on the evangelical nature of hospitality. We read the scriptures in light of hospitality, we slanted our ministries toward hospitality, we invited our congregation to experiment with hospitality—openness to the stranger, welcoming the outsider, befriending the friendless and those in need. But it's only now, years later, that we see those taught habits becoming instinct—perhaps even virtue.

On Monday, Jim confided in me about the ways he and his wife have felt compelled to help a troubled employee. They're crossing the line of standard business practice. They've involved their hearts, and it's costing them—far more than money. Jim said nothing about the sermons he may have heard years before. He didn't cite the language of hospitality that's had currency among our congregation. "We couldn't turn our backs this time," is all Jim knew how to say. "She is in need and we have the means to help. We don't really know what we're doing. We do not know where this is going. But we can't shake the sense that this is what the Lord wants done."

On Wednesday, a woman told me of her awakening to Jesus Christ. In middle age, and long alienated from the church and organized religion, she's found herself irresistibly drawn near because of the way of life of a few people who've been present to her through several crises. She never heard any of our congregation's sermons on the

God who welcomes the stranger, listens to the angry, sits among the dispossessed. She couldn't have known about the ways we've altered our ministries to create habits of openness. But she did experience the presence of those who had heard these sermons and are now giving room for her questions, listening to her anger, and speaking of God with her without manipulation.

Then on Friday, Michael, a professor at the university, told me of the way he and his wife, along with over half a dozen other disciples from our congregation, had mobilized to give a safe place and a truthful perspective to a student caught up in a dangerous way of life. None of these would say that what they're doing is because of the sermons our preachers preached during that year's focus on hospitality. I don't even think these people would call what they're doing "hospitality." And some of them might even be tempted from time to time to say, "What ever happened to that focus we had a few years ago on hospitality? Why don't we have a mission or core values statement that says something about that?"

What's important is that those sermons, now long forgotten, have seeded what our congregation's now doing. The Word spoken, established values and habits now become instincts (maybe even real virtues)—the source of which they can no longer identify. The people of God are now acting on an inner necessity, a nudge, a compulsion planted and nurtured by the ministry of the Word, and it's they, not the preacher, who are practicing the sermon.

35

If Your Sermon's a Dog, Walk It Proudly

We can't always preach as well as we'd like to. We may well want to soar with the angels every Sunday, but to do so would demand too much of the equipment we're given. We are human, gloriously and scandalously so. And gloriously and scandalously, God has entrusted the Word to us . . . Sunday after Sunday. That means there will be times when we may well feel closer to hell than to heaven, but we've got to preach anyway. From hell. In our poverty and weakness and humiliation. We won't see it at times like these, but there's a certain glory in preaching from near hell itself—maybe more glory than when we're flying close to heaven. The glory of God was *there*, right there, in the humiliation of our Lord Jesus . . . and it'll be there in ours.

None of us wants to preach poorly, but frankly, none of us can avoid it. There are times when nothing seems to be working right—our thinking's muddled, our exegesis shallow, our sense of the pastoral focus of the text is, well, anything but focused. We seem to preach all over the map and worry that we say very little that's helpful. In times like these no amount of hard work will pull things together.

That happened to me on Sunday. The liturgy was jam-packed. Special musicians. Youth confirmation. Eucharist. And at one of the services we also baptized. Somewhere in the midst of all this I was supposed to preach. With that much to plan and coordinate during the week and, adding to that, the heaviness dropped into the week by pastoral crises, I never did find the kind of rhythm I generally need to prepare the sermon. When I rose to preach, I stumbled over words—my mind muddled with too many details, my exegesis rootless from little study, and my sense of pastoral focus scattered at best. I know I said something about the text (but I don't know what), then pressed myself through the sacraments, and sat down wishing I'd written something out. I also cursed myself for allowing too much into the service in the first place, criticizing my liturgical judgment and leadership of our worship team.

I'd wanted to soar, but I'd stumbled around on the floor. Today, I can better see why—I'd lost sight of what gives me freedom, and I'd lost sight of what gives the Word freedom among the people of the Word.

Throughout this book I write about this kind of free-dom, but old habits die hard, and I, myself, have to keep reading my own testimony. Preaching like I did on Sunday helped me recover and make explicit today another lesson I've learned along the way: a way of preaching that inches me toward real freedom—and true glory—when there's very little I can do to soar toward the glory I think I want, and instead feel so ignominiously grounded to the earth.

Once, when fretting through a pre-dawn Sunday morning, trying to press a little more production from my intellectual equipment, hoping to push away that inner gnawing that what I had to offer in a few hours was little more than straw, I heard this little whisper in my head, "Go ahead, Chris, preach as badly as you can. You can't do it." And I laughed . . . for the first time ever on a Sunday morning—a great hilarious, free, joyous kind of laugh that I'd not known was possible as a preacher.

Of course! Try to preach badly! Fling yourself out past all your efforts to preach well, and you'll be free. Gloriously free. Short-circuit the anxious brooding over performance. Stop trying to be good. Cease needing to soar. And try, instead, to be bad—even as bad as you can be—and being bad is an impossibility. Do this, and you'll enter into a freedom God can work with. You'll be free to be in the room, present to the moment, listening for the Word now, a mystic preacher. Going there may not replicate the flights of the angels or those super-communicators whose public image bullies us with superstar glory. But if the gospel's got anything to say about preaching, I've got a hunch it wants to tell us that we'll find glory when we feel least holy, least competent, stupid, close to the mud of earth, even the darkness of hell. But it's from such mud that we were formed by the breath, the Word of God.

So, go ahead, preach as badly as you can when something's clipped your wings and you can't find a way to fly. You can't preach badly if preaching badly's your aim.

Students stare at me incredulously when I talk this way, so I often put it another way. "If your sermon's a dog," I tell them, "walk it proudly." And then they laugh (a rarity in the preaching classroom). It's that ability to laugh that I'm after. Laughter frees us up for the kind of joy that the world needs from our preaching.

It would have been good for me to remember that last Sunday morning as I stewed over my mistakes. I've preached plenty of sermons when I didn't soar with the angels—sermons that were real dogs. But when I was fortunate to remember that little whisper, "Go ahead, Chris, preach as badly as you can; I dare you," I've never preached a bad sermon.

There's something really right about this theologically. Preach as badly as you can, walk your dog proudly, embrace the *humus* of your human life, and it just might be that down here, on earth—not in the heavens—that we actually do the most good. When we preach what we think is bad (and give ourselves to the grace of going there), not only will we experience true freedom, but we will touch true glory—a joy itself that is the real gift of the gospel—and our people may find themselves face to face with a testimony that speaks them toward the presence and glory and *joy* of God when they themselves find that they're living in the mud.

Sunday
A Prayer before the Word

On Jeremiah 1; 1 Samuel 4:10–22
May 29, 2005
On the day of Elizabeth Wilson's ordination

It's easy to want more than you are willing to give.
We want signs and wonders,
proof positive that it is you who will back us up—
and mightily—
when we step out in daring obedience.

We imagine Jeremiah wanting more,
. . . and this dying mother in the Samuel text,
. . . and Liz too on this day of her ordination.

But the truth is, most of us serve you well
    and bravely,
not because of signs and wonders
    and lifetime warranties
but because we live by faith—
faith that trusts in these texts of yours,
faith in the testimony of those gone before,
faith in words that oftentimes seem so
puny, fragile, and weak
against the larger and louder and grander things
    of this world.

But for us, words are enough—
even whispers are enough—

to give us hope, and inch us past our Friday fears,
through our Saturday muteness,
and into the Sunday courage
    you have in mind for us.

So give us a few good words again today,
and we will once again be your sent people—
Eastered for the gospel's ministry in the world.

Amen.

36

"Do Not Be Afraid":
Whispers Remembered
as You Begin Your Ministry

1 Samuel 4:10–22 ✝ Upon the Ordination of Elizabeth Wilson
Minister of Word and Sacrament ✝ Sunday, May 29, 2005

1. We send you out into a changed world

We, the congregation that's helped form you, are sending you out into a changed world. It is not the world it was even thirty years ago when this congregation began its adventure together. The world is not what it was ten years ago, or five. It is not what it was last year or even yesterday.

There was a time when we believed we understood with a fair amount of accuracy the North American world into which we send seminary graduates like you. There was a time when we believed we knew how to prepare future pastors for roles that were pretty predictable. But this world in recent years has entered a dizzying period of change, or, more accurately, a period of radical upheaval, which has made us much less certain that we know what we are doing and how to adequately prepare you for the mission of Jesus Christ. We in the North American church are recognizing that the stable world of Christendom, in which the church knew its role as chaplain to society, is crumbling. The church is no longer the center of Western culture, and the gospel that was once so influential is, at best, no longer interesting and, at worst, viewed as archaic and sometimes hostile to people wanting to build a new world. There is little doubt that we are now living through a period of unprecedented global change.

This is the world into which we send you, and there's not one of us who doesn't pray we've done all that we can to make you ready.

Make no mistake, the adventure you now commence will demand the best of you. The world will not always be kind to you. It will not always welcome you. It will not always treat you with respect. You may not always have a soft pillow, or a full stomach, or a healthy body and mind. No, the mission before you will not be easy. But that's not what you signed up for when you signed on with Jesus Christ, is it? An easy life is not worthy of your gifts. An easy life is not worthy of your energy, your intellect, your life, your death.

Have no illusions; there are powers at work in the world that will oppose everything you stand for. They are forceful, frightening, malevolent, dangerous, dark. They will seek to swallow you and the optimism and hope that are yours on this day. You will stand at the grave of one killed tragically, and you will wonder. You will face such hostility from those you serve that you will question. You will feel things in your own soul and flesh that will plunge you into the pit of despair. You will see things in this world that will make you doubt everything.

So, as you begin your ministry, we want to whisper one thing into you, for there is only one thing that really matters.

2. When death is all people know

Reading from 1 Samuel 4 is surely not common at ordinations. It's not bright and airy, the kind of text we generally want at times like this when we want to send you out with light in your eyes and wind at your back. This passage is dark and fearsome, but not entirely. And that's why I've chosen it to offer to you today. I think it is just the right kind of reading for today.

It is the right kind of text to bind to your heart and mind, to preach over you, to pray into you. It's obscure enough to stay in your memory, if for no other reason than that you remember the crazy pastor who preached it over you on the day of your ordination. But I think you'll find that it whispers to you over and over again over the years. It will whisper to you not just in the bright and airy times when remembering the gospel is easy, but more importantly it will whisper to you when life is darkest, at just that point in time when remembering the gospel is the most difficult thing to do—for you and those you serve. This word, I trust, will save you over and over again as you remember what is whispered here.

The people who have long cherished this text from Samuel know that it is a story about a world swept into massive upheaval and crisis. It is a pastoral text. It names people's deep sense of loss. It names people's fears, confusion, and anxiety over the future. It is utterly realistic about the fragility of life. And it speaks about all this in a very loud voice, the kind of voice people inside and outside our churches hear most of the time. But it also whispers the kind of word of hope upon which frightened people build the future, the kind of whisper that makes biblical people relentlessly hopeful in spite of desperate circumstances.

In a loud voice it tells us that thirty thousand of Israel's troops were slaughtered by the Philistines on that day. The husbands and fathers and sons of many, many women in Israel lie dead. And not only are these women filled with grief, they are full of fear. This is not only a personal crisis of grief; this is a public crisis of national security. You cannot overestimate the pain and fear felt by this community. It is the most severe kind of pastoral crisis any of us can face. It is September 11, 2001, but on a massive scale. What's more, the ark of God has been captured.

The ark of God is not merely a religious symbol, nor is it a symbol of national pride—it is not the same as the attack on our Pentagon. The ark *is* the presence of Yahweh. Where the ark goes, Yahweh goes. The ark, now in the hands of Israel's enemies, means that *Yahweh* is in exile. This is terribly hard for us to imagine, and we Christians would like to correct the story at this point; we know that God is not kept in a box. But we cannot edit the text to fit our understanding, for the story wants to paint the completeness of the frightful changes that have swept Israel into crisis.

What this text describes here on a national scale is what you may at some point in your ministry experience when someone, wrenched into grief by the death of a child, says to you, "There is no God. God has abandoned me."

The news of the battle comes to Eli, who has served as priest over Israel for forty years. The text tells us that he is ninety-eight years old and blind. He is waiting for news. Perhaps he is already filled with dread, as we often are when in our guts we know there's something to dread even before our minds know the facts. The messenger delivers his grim report. "Israel has fled before the Philistines, and there has also been a great slaughter among the troops; your two sons also, Hophni and Phinehas, are dead." It gets worse, of course, and the messenger saves the worst for last. *"And the ark of God has been captured."*

At these words, the text is careful to tell us, Eli collapses. Falling from his priestly chair, breaking his neck. The men are slaughtered. God is captured. The priest is dead.

3. You are to fix your attention on something astonishingly small

At this, the text turns its attention to the drama of a single, pregnant woman. How astonishing! Amid these grand geopolitical themes rises this little, but oh-so-carefully told story of a pregnant woman and the birth of her child. And we who've read the rest of the Bible instinctively know that this small thing is no small thing—for at another time when the events of the larger world seemed so terribly important comes another story of a pregnant woman thrown into childbirth. And we know that *that* story is the story that whispers salvation to the world.

Notice that this particular text gives no name for this woman. She is known only as Eli's "daughter-in-law," "the wife of Phinehas." Defined by the males of her world, this

185

woman and her womb will do what those males in all their power cannot do. And of course (as is always true of those who are used by God to birth something gospel, something missional), she is quite unaware of her power—her body seems powerless and puny in comparison to the machines of war and the craft of global politics.

(I can't help but wonder if those first disciples of Jesus might have liked this little text. Defined by the power of Rome, they knew they were so puny and weak. Hardly capable of the mission Jesus had entrusted to them . . . but if they knew this text, they knew otherwise.)

The text tells us that "upon hearing the news that the ark of God was captured, and that her father-in-law and husband are dead," she is thrown into premature childbirth. It looks as if death is going to be the only word spoken in Israel on this dark day. Dying, she delivers a child. And as she dies, her lips mouth these final words to those around her: "Ichabod," which means, "Where is the glory?" "Call the boy Ichabod," she says. "The glory has departed Israel, for the ark of God has been captured." Ichabod is not a good name for a child. But on this day, it is the only word she and perhaps so many women in Israel know how to speak.

4. Dare to whisper the words from which a whole new world is born

But there are a few other women in Israel that day, and I like to think that they are the reason this text lives on in the memory of God's people. This text lives on not because of the way it names the darkness and desperation of the times, the bewildering changes that break in among us, scattering our confidence. It lives on not because a

186

poor boy was named cruelly according to his mother's despair. No, this text lives on because a few unnamed midwives dared to live in contrast to all that was going on around them, a few unnamed, newly ordained preachers dared to whisper different words in the darkest of times, a few pastors and the congregations who received their words dared to define their lives evangelically—they refused to define the world according to the ways of death so potent. They dared to whisper news that points us to a new power being delivered into the world. They dared to trust in the mischief of God.

"As she was about to die," the story goes, "the women attending her said to her, 'Do not be afraid, for you have borne a son.'" We've heard those words before, echoed so many centuries later, into a new night of fear and despair.

> "A child is born to us; a son is given!" "Do not be afraid!"

A baby, so fragile, born under the shadow of death, caught in the hands of a few unnamed midwives.

> "A child is born to us; a son is given!" "Do not be afraid!"

A baby, guarantee of the future and of life's relentless power over death. A baby, adored by the simple. Welcomed by the humble.

> "A child is born to us; a son is given!" "Do not be afraid!"

Oh, the wonder! The power of those words, whispered once and then again, and so many times since! That little whisper that undoes death's work. That one little whisper, more powerful than all the designs and devices of the mighty. That one little whisper that bends all creation toward life.

And you—oh, the wonder of it all!—you, Elizabeth, and us with you, are witnesses of these things. We are stewards of these wonders, and *you* are made an apostle of this Word.

We've prepared you as best we can for this work. And now, with this text tucked into your memory, we charge you, little unsung preacher, midwife of the Word, sent wherever God now scatters you—Shout the Word! Celebrate the Word! Live the Word! Dance the Word! Know the Word! Love the Word! Teach the Word! Pray the Word! Cradle the Word! Cherish the Word! Carry the Word! Trust the Word! And when some force comes against you and you cannot do these things, when you and your people are afraid—by all means, by hook and by crook, whatever it takes, *whisper* the Word!

It is the only thing that really matters.

It is on this Word—even (maybe especially!) if it must be *whispered* under your breath—that empires topple and God's new world is born.

—◈—

A note on sermon delivery: Including this sermon manuscript may confuse some readers. In these pages, I tell you that I very rarely carry a manuscript with me when preaching. Neither do I memorize the sermon. But I have said that I *do* write sermons (or commentaries on the text, or parts of sermons). It's this writing of the sermon that most helps me order my thoughts, and it's the way I divide the sermon and mark its breaks with descriptive and memorable section headers that helps me gather the sermon inside my heart on Saturday evening and then keep close to my work come Sunday morning:

1. We send you out into a changed world.
2. When death is all people know,
3. You are to fix your attention on something astonishingly small,
4. And dare to whisper the words from which a whole new world is born.

The sermon I actually preach is often pretty close to what I've written, not because I've memorized it, but because it's now become part of me and I've found a sermon form that enables me to order the material for delivery while giving me ample room to improvise in the moment.

37

Preaching Naked

A friend once asked me how long it takes for me to prepare a sermon. She was curious about how many hours I spent in study and writing during the week. Some preachers spend as little as an hour or two a week, others as much as thirty. I felt a bit playful at the time and unreflectively blurted out, "a lifetime . . . nothing less, nothing more!" Over the years, I've come to realize just how true that playful response was. A preacher preaches out of a lifetime of journeying with God, learning to hear and obey the Word of God, letting that Word rumble around inside, confronting darkness with God's light, lifting the soul into the eternal mystery of the Trinity. I want my preaching to flow from me like water from a fresh spring—bubbling up from inside me with freedom, joy, transparency, vulnerability, courage, and passion.

To get to that place in any given week, I've had to linger for six full days in the text, asking questions of the Bible passage I'm going to preach on Sunday; and, of course, turnabout's fair play—I also want to allow the text its own time to interrogate me, the congregation, and the world. Without this exchange I remain in control and avoid the life-changing (sometimes crushing, sometimes healing) power of the God whose Word is "like fire . . . and like a hammer that breaks a rock in pieces" (Jeremiah 23:29), or like bread to the hungry (Matthew 4:4) and light to those who walk in darkness (Psalm 119:105).

From what I've written throughout this book regarding "exegesis for preachers on the run," you know that I spend anywhere from six to ten hours a week in fairly intense study and writing, Monday through Friday mornings. Then, by Friday afternoon, I've put those written notes into a binder and let them go, entering into a twenty-four-plus-hour Friday/Saturday season away from specific sermon preparation. As I spend time with my family on Friday night and Saturday, doing chores around the house, or playing out in the community, the Word soaks into my soul, and the texture of daily life meets that Word in all of its freedom and mischief. By Saturday night I'm ready to pray through the text again, remembering what I've written in the past, but this time pulling it all forward into the moment, and letting God shape me so that I can open the text among my people in worship the next morning in such a way that we all encounter the living, speaking God.

Now, having come this far with you, this leads me to comment on what I call "preaching naked"—that is, without a written sermon, or with only a few sketchy notes.

Preaching is not a literary event. It's essentially oral in nature. Jesus did not slave over a written manuscript

191

before he delivered the Sermon on the Mount. Paul probably did not deliver a written speech to the Athenians. Such truths do not necessarily mean we shouldn't. But this does open me to the possibility of another way. In African village congregations, I often didn't know I was preaching until after the worship service had already started; they expected that a preacher could preach *ex tempore*, that is, from a life lived with the text and with a message that came "from the moment."

Perhaps it's not strange that I learned this in Africa—even the most famous and influential of African preachers, St. Augustine (late fourth century), preached extemporaneously. In his book *Augustine of Hippo: Sermons to the People,* William Griffin tell us that Augustine's practice was to go about his day pondering the biblical text he would host the next day in worship. He would focus his message by taking the text for his meditations and prayers the night before. Then when "it came time for him to speak, with no notes, no prepared text, as was the custom of the time, he delivered it *ex tempore.* . . . Because he always preached on [biblical] materials that were dear to his heart, he was never at a loss for words."

I wonder if it's not a luxury of life lived during those years of an essentially Christian Europe and North America that preachers could write and deliver carefully crafted sermons/lectures to highly biblically literate congregations. Those days are over, and we are living once again in an essentially missionary setting. In this post-Christian, postmodern setting, I think what people most need is not oratory, but authentic witness.

Søren Kierkegaard was an earnest Danish Christian who believed that the church had simply sold out to culture and, being too much like the culture, consequently could not offer a genuine Christian witness to that culture. Over a hundred years ago he spoke words that preachers today need to heed:

> The person who is going to preach ought to live in the Christian thoughts and ideas; they ought to be his daily life. If so, and this is the view of Christianity—then you, too, will have eloquence enough and precisely that which is needed when you speak extemporaneously without specific preparation. However, it is a fallacious eloquence if someone, without otherwise occupying himself with, without living in these thoughts, once in a while sits down and laboriously collects such thoughts, perhaps in the field of literature, and then works them into a well-composed discourse, which is then committed to memory and delivered superbly, with respect both to voice and diction and to gestures. No, just as in well equipped houses one need not go downstairs to fetch water but has it up there on tap, under pressure—one merely turns on the faucet—so also is that person an authentic Christian speaker who, because the essentially Christian is his life, at every moment has eloquence present, immediately available, precisely the true eloquence. . . . If your life expresses what you heard, your eloquence is more powerful, more true, more persuasive than all the art of orators. (*For Self Examination,* in the Introductory Note)

This authentic witness is what people today are searching for. Most of us are suspicious of the impersonal and inauthentic. In our high-tech, media-saturated, excellence-in-presentation age, we're longing for simplicity and integrity, for a look-me-in-the-eye-and-tell-me-as-you-see-it witness to God's coming to us in Jesus Christ.

Preaching the way I do is my attempt to be as authentic as I can possibly be. Others will find their own way, and for them it may well be preaching from a manuscript. In fact, I've taught students who came from extemporaneous preaching traditions but who found their true preaching selves in the preparation and preaching of a written text.

The key, as far as I'm concerned, is finding a way that fits for the way each preacher is made. David, the shepherd boy, determined to face Goliath, knew that he'd get himself killed if he tried to wear Saul's armor. He wisely knew he must go out armed only with what was authentic to David's way of being David.

38

Mystic Preaching

Earlier, I invited you to consider preaching as an art or experience more like that of a musician than that of a lecturer. I'd explored the way U2's Bono understands what he and the band are up to in their music. About my comparison between the work of the preacher and the performance of U2, fellow preacher Beth Maynard once told me: "What fascinates me is Bono's ability to get himself in character, inhabiting the songs for the sake of the audience (not unlike a preacher who inhabits the gospel message for the sake of the congregation), while also communicating humanness and vulnerability, not so much by what he says about the songs he sings as by who he is and how he sings them."

Beth's language of "inhabiting" the songs—or for us preachers, inhabiting the text—moves preaching in the right direction. I can't speak for Bono and his singing, but

I can speak to my own experience and what inhabiting the text has meant to me. There is a form of inhabiting the text that happens to me with enough infrequency that I long for more, but frequently enough that I am grateful when it comes.

What I'm talking about I can speak of only in mystical terms. There is a zone, a spiritual state that can occur in preaching that is similar to the experience testified to by warriors, who in the midst of battle are caught up in the battle spirit, and time stands still and they enter into a new state of being entirely. Alternatively, it is like the experience of a cellist who finds herself suddenly in a moment in which she has transcended all her technique and training and is one with the music, in harmony with that divine song that holds the universe together. She is no longer speaking instructions to herself and playing a score; rather, she is being played.

I don't know that what I am describing is an ecstatic experience so much as it is mystical. It is not irrational; the mind is still alert—even uncommonly alert. In preaching moments like these I am uncharacteristically calm, fully present to the moment, reverent to something greater than myself, astonishingly open, free. I imagine Bono and the band find themselves in this place when somewhere into a song they realize that they are no longer making the music, the music is making them. They are no longer playing to an audience. Time has stood still. There is no past and there is no future. There is only now. Only the song. And all—band and listener—are involved in something much bigger than themselves.

There is for me a way of preaching that loosens itself from the heightened rational faculties we're all so good with and enters into a simplicity of focus, freedom, relinquishment, and abandonment in which I as preacher am not preaching at people, not for people, but we are together in the moment. And while I may be the one speaking, I have become the voice of us all, and the voice of Jesus Christ who is for and among us all. I also know from experience that it is my anxiety or grinding away or trying too hard to be good that gums up the equipment God's given me—some quite remarkable equipment, which when surrendered can become a vehicle for revelation.

This does not mean I do not prepare a sermon, any more than it means that a violinist doesn't practice or that U2 doesn't rehearse. It means hard preparatory work so that I know my chords, the score, the text, the moves. But it means that when it comes time to deliver, I'm not bringing something from the study so much as I have been prepared for this moment and that now, right now, I must listen, listen, listen in reverence and awe before the Almighty whose Word is right here, all around and among us. With this text as guardian and guide, I must pull the Word out of the air and from among the people, and from those deep, scripture-formed places, Spirit-drenched places within my own soul and the soul of the congregation around me.

It is a dance in the Mystery. It is being naked and unafraid. It is electric, an inhabiting of the Holy. A being inhabited by the Holy. It is no performance. No game. No charade. No manufacturing of religious experience. I've come to wonder if this isn't what Jesus meant when he told his simple little preachers, "Do not worry about how you are to defend yourselves or what you are to say; for the Holy Spirit will teach you at that very hour what you are to say" (Luke 12:11–12).

While *mystical* does not appear in the New Testament, *mystery* does. Both words are related to the verb *myein*, "to close," that is, to close the eyes or lips and express what is seen or heard in secret. I'm not a scholar of mysticism—though from what I know, mysticism is a universal human experience, and it's held a vital place within the most vibrant expressions of Christianity. But to my knowledge it's not been much explored in the church's preaching. Maybe that's because it's not easy to control or to understand. I don't think it ever will be; and maybe that's a good thing.

I do know that it's come to me. I've tasted it. So have the preachers we're training in our congregation. So have my students at the seminary. But preaching this way, this mystical inhabiting of the Word, is fragile. Self-doubt, fear, insecurity can scatter it, like a wild hare in the woods before the clumsy boots of a careless teenager. A good deal of the time, I preach this way, rather clumsily. And even clumsy's good enough. Maybe on a regular basis, it's even better. Expecting to enter the Mystery always is too much for the equipment we're given; what's more, it would tempt us to believe we can control what is thankfully beyond our powers. We ought never to have that kind of control. Mystic preaching would cease being a gift and would become a terrible power to wield.

39

Learning to Enter Sabbath— A Preacher's Sunday

Sabbath is not about resting so that we can be ready to work again. It's not a day-long vacation dressed in religious garb. Sabbath ensures that we don't make ourselves gods. It keeps God and us and creation rightly related and rightly ordered. I'm not good at keeping Sabbath, and for that reason I don't think I'm good (yet) at being human—I get brittle, pushy, greedy, sometimes too sure of myself, other times too insecure. I wound myself and wound others. I get so caught up in what I'm doing that I can't see that I've become a captive. Full humanness is more than what I'm living.

I was once reading the first chapter of Genesis and came to the text that says, "God saw everything that he had made, and indeed, it was very good" (v. 31). At those words, suddenly into my brain sprang the words, "But *you* say, 'It's never good enough!'" Never good enough.

Always more to be done. And for me, up until recently, it was always I who had to do it. The musician Quincy Jones once lamented learning all this too late—only after his drive had ruined his three marriages.

Life without Sabbath, wounds. Preachers too often live out-of-control lives, and it makes me tremble to think what our Sabbathless lives can do to others. Without some kind of Sabbath—a place where we break completely from the grind—we might well lose our own souls even while preaching to others.

The rhythm of my week means Saturday is my day off. On Saturday I help clean the house, work in the yard, grocery shop, balance the checkbook, walk with my wife to the Great Harvest Bread store down the street. Saturday is not my Sabbath. It is a different workday. I do all this on Saturday so that come Sunday I *can* practice Sabbath, along with the congregation who claims me. Most pastors I know cannot conceive of Sunday as Sabbath—"it is our workday," they say. I disagree. It is the church's day of worship, of reflection, of holy rest. Choral members sing on Sunday, Sunday school teachers teach, volunteers turn on lights and unlock doors and pick up trash on the lawn, worship leaders pray and give announcements. We are all involved in the actions of worship. And I'm no different. I preach and perhaps do a few other things. It's true, we pastors may worship *more* (most Sundays, three different services for me), but worship, even leading in worship, is not like the work I do the other six days of the week. It's what Christians *do* on the Sabbath—engage God and dwell among the people of God in peculiar and intentional ways. Since I've practiced Sabbath this way, my Sunday experience is profoundly different, and I'm free on Saturday to do a little work here and there and not be angry about it. I put my head to the pillow on Saturday night, having engaged the text again and prayed through the next day, with a sense of peace mingled with mild expectation. Our congregation too is learning to practice Sabbath and practice Sunday in new ways. There is an increasing sense that not only is Sabbath critical for our future, it is an essential practice that witnesses to the ways of the God we love and serve. Without it, we are in danger of becoming merely activist. What the church most needs in the future is wisdom, love born from seeking the face of God (Psalm 27:8), the clear eye of spiritual depth. And for this, the church's future requires a recovery of the Christian practice of leisure, holy rest, resistance to the stress-filled work world around us that endeavors to push us 24/7. On Sundays we worship God, we talk with one another in the narthex and on the patio, we take walks, sit on the porch, linger on the phone, smell roses, read books, listen to music, pray. I am now among them. And it makes a world of difference.

When I am old I want to have come to the place where I really do believe that the world is not my responsibility. Sure, I want to know that I've had a role in what the world's come to be. But I also want to know that over the long haul of my life there's been this Presence—hovering, moving, luring, laughing, rumbling, wooing, doing things I've not controlled, managed, or dreamed up. I guess I'm wagering that practicing Sabbath over the long haul will check the compulsive and presumptive ways that might otherwise have characterized my work. I'm also trusting that by saying no once a week to all that seeks to claim my life and keep me endlessly busy, I might, by life's end, have actually become human—learning to laugh and smile and love. I suppose that when I die I want to have gotten that right. Sabbath, shared with my people, helps me toward that end.

40

Why You Must Not Work Too Hard

Over 31% of college-educated male workers are regularly logging 50 or more hours a week at work, up from 22% in 1980. About 40% of American adults get less than seven hours of sleep on weekdays, up from 34% in 2001. Almost 60% of meals are rushed, and 34% of lunches are choked down on the run. To avoid wasting time, we're talking on our cell phones while rushing to work, answering e-mails during conference calls, waking up at 4 a.m. to call Europe and generally multitasking our brains out.

BusinessWeek, October 3, 2005

That's the bad news, the good news is that there's something new afoot. Business leaders are recognizing that their lives, driven by work, are out of control. More and more of them are learning ways to flip the "off" switch. Says Paul Saffo, a director at the Institute for the Future, a think tank based in Palo Alto, California: "Solitude is the scarce resource in business lives—having that time when you are disconnected and realize that everything will go along fine without you." One top-level executive has given up cell phones and computers, saying, "I never had time to think." Another says, "Now I make sure there's at least one day when I don't even touch a keyboard" (*BusinessWeek*).

The modern world is collapsing, and a new one is being born. Many Americans are growing suspicious of the modern assumptions that drive us to work harder, produce more, and spend more time at work. They're discovering that modernity did not finally free us but has made us captives of the totalitarian regime of industry—a life consumed by work. In the midst of this collapse, there are leaders who are learning to recover the reflective space to do the mental and spiritual work necessary to form the kinds of communities—business and social—whose intellectual and moral life is born of the wisdom necessary for the twenty-first century.

Will we preachers who lead the church, we who form it with our words, have what it takes for those words to be born of the wisdom our congregations and world need in the days ahead?

I've lived long inside the decades of modernity's last gasp, and so have you. Frankly, my work ethic is catechized more by modernity than by the church's history. I, for one, am coming up against the bankruptcy of this ethic both professionally and personally. Professionally, I see the dangers of perpetuating congregational life built on the sand of Kant's ethic of "Herculean labor." Our people are often more modern than they are Christian, and their practice of time offers no real witness to God's alternative kingdom, to the truth that in Jesus Christ we possess all the time in the world—we have eternal life. And personally, my entrance into middle age and a life lived with chronic disease (one that is exaggerated by stress) both mean that I can no longer continue this pace of life and live well—or perhaps, live at all. The wear and tear on my physical, intellectual, and spiritual equipment means that I can no longer achieve by sheer effort and act of the will what I once produced. The mind and soul often feel gummed up. Working the equipment harder no longer ensures the outcomes it once did. And unless I change, something's bound to break inside me. Unless I change, I not only will be unable to lead our congregation into the future God has for it, but will actually hinder our growth in godliness, because the congregation will lack a witness that can help free it from the gridlock of a way of life that values the excessively active even while it becomes increasingly shallow and strange to the kind of wisdom required of us now.

Yes, I am a witness; so are you. But to what and to whom?

In the year 590 CE, upon the death of Pope Pelagius II, Gregory, the abbot of St. Andrew's Monastery in Rome was called to become the new pope—the church's chief pastor and preacher. He did not want the job and "undertook the burden of the dignity with a sick heart." He wanted a life of contemplation and prayer, perceiving that a life spent cultivating a clear eye of faith, the wisdom won only by a perpetual seeking of the face of God (Psalm 27:8), was the most important contribution he could offer to his turbulent world.

It was a time of great transition, a hinge between the collapse of Rome and the ceding of its mighty empire to another. Gregory, the wise abbot, knew that those troubled times did not need more busy pastors. It did not want more harried preachers whose words were shallow. It could not be helped by more administrators who loved positions of influence and who wanted the power to get things done. And yet, he also knew that the church in the world needed formation for its witness to Jesus Christ. It needed his wisdom. It needed his voice. But more, if it was to be the church, vibrant in witness, it needed the wise voices of its preachers scattered throughout the world.

Too long had those preachers been formed by Roman imperial versions of their work. The church's pastors had long been schooled in forms of leadership that would not and could not sustain the church as the witness to Christ. And so, he wrote his little rule for clergy, *Liber Regulae Pastoralis* (Pastoral Care). What St. Benedict's rule had done for monastics, St. Gregory did for pastors. And in that rule, Gregory wrote:

> Often it happens that when a man undertakes the cares of government, his heart is distracted with a diversity of things, and as his mind is divided among many interests and becomes confused, he finds he is unfitted for any of them. This is why a certain wise man gives a cautious warning, saying: "My son, meddle not with many matters" (Ecclesiasticus 11:10).

Fourteen hundred years later, we're not far off from St. Gregory's world. Busyness endangers the soul. Administrative responsibilities have consumed the lives of those who are sent to host the Word of God among the people of God. Busyness and power endanger congregations who are themselves sent into the world as preaching congregations, hosting the Word of God in the world.

"Meddle not with many matters," St. Gregory counseled his preachers, and for this wisdom, he himself reached back into another time, 200 BCE, and to *The Wisdom of Ben Sirach,* or *Ecclesiasticus,* a pastoral tract sketched up in that cosmopolitan city of Alexandria, where rabbis were teaching their ministers of the Word how to form congregations loyal to the God of the Bible rather than the gods of Egypt or Greece or Rome.

So, preacher, go ahead, "meddle not with many matters." Learn to flip the "off" switch. Take time to think, doodle, play. If you don't, your congregation will lack the kind of witness who can help free it from the gridlock of a way of life that values the excessively active, the spiritually shallow. But if you do, you'll be the kind of witness the church and this world most need, and you'll help preach us all toward the freedom we were made to enjoy.

Brazos Press is grounded in the ancient, ecumenical Christian tradition, understood as living and dynamic. As legend has it, Brazos is the Spanish name explorers gave to a prominent Texas river upon seeing how its winding waters sustained fertile soil in an arid land. They christened this life-giving channel Los Brazos de Dios, "the arms of God."

Our logo connotes a river with multiple currents all flowing in the same direction, just as the major streams of the Christian tradition are various but all surging from and to the same God. The logo's three "streams" also reflect the Trinitarian God who lives and gives life at the heart of all true Christian faith.

Our books are marketed and distributed intensively and broadly through the American Booksellers Association and the Christian Booksellers networks and bookstores; national chains and independent bookstores; Catholic and mainline bookstores; and library and international markets. We are a division of Baker Publishing Group.

Brazos Book Club and Border Crossings

Brazos books help people grapple with the important issues of the day and make Christian sense of pervasive issues in the church, academy, and contemporary world. Our authors engage such topics as spirituality, the arts, the economy, popular culture, theology, biblical studies, the social sciences, and more. At both the popular and academic levels, we publish books by evangelical, Roman Catholic, Protestant mainline, and Eastern Orthodox authors.

If you'd like to join the Brazos Book Club and receive our books upon publication at book club prices, please sign up online at **www.brazospress.com/brazosbookclub**.

To sign up for our monthly email newsletter, Border Crossings, visit **www.brazospress.com**. This email newsletter provides information on upcoming and recently released books, conferences we are attending, and more.

Brazos Press
The Tradition Alive